101

Tips for Winning
More Tennis Matches

Michael Kosta

**COACHES
≡ CHOICE**™

ISBN: 978-1-58518-989-2
Library of Congress Control Number: 2006930476
Book layout: Bean Creek Studio
Cover design: Studio J Art & Design
Front cover photo: Courtesy of University of Illinois Sports Information
Author photo: ©UM Photo Services, Martin Vloet

Coaches Choice
P.O. Box 1828
Monterey, CA 93942
www.coacheschoice.com

Dedication

This book is dedicated to Christian Amedia, my junior doubles partner, who left us too early and never had the opportunity to fulfill his tennis dreams.

Acknowledgments

This book, along with my entire professional career, would never have happened without the support of everyone involved with Tennis Investors, L.L.C. You allowed me to pursue a dream and I will cherish that forever. Thank you.

My parents share a remarkable enthusiasm for their children's lives. Without that enthusiasm, this book would have never made it. Thank you for not only making junior, college, and professional tennis possible, but for keeping me motivated and smiling along the way.

Craig and Bruce, you both challenged me to get better and showed me how through your own discipline and effort. Some of my best memories involve competing with and for you both. Thank you for spending the time to teach us properly. Bruce, it is a privilege to work with you. Thank you for the opportunity.

Many thanks go to John, Kristy, and Todd. Each of you support my tennis in different but equal ways. You've always been my number one fans and I cherish that.

I have been fortunate to have great teammates, friends, and coaches help me with my tennis and this book. Thanks for always making it fun.

Tom Hackett did a fantastic job polishing the original manuscript (all 120,000 words). Thank you.

Contents

    Tip #1: Stencil your rackets.
    Tip #2: Look nice for matches.
    Tip #3: Know your mental balance.
    Tip #4: Do the "belly button" test.
    Tip #5: Prepare on-court food and drink.
    Tip #6: Serve out your match the night before.
    Tip #7: Shoot free throws like Michael Jordan.
    Tip #8: Include protein in your breakfast.
    Tip #9: Learn nasal breathing and the sun salutation.

    Tip #10: Introduce yourself to your opponent.
    Tip #11: Wear two pairs of socks.
    Tip #12: Accept the weather.
    Tip #13: Take a 30-second regroup before starting a tiebreaker.
    Tip #14: Never miss returns.
    Tip #15: Serve into the body on big points.
    Tip #16: Lob high when on the run.
    Tip #17: Loosen your grip.
    Tip #18: Hit low volleys behind your opponent and high volleys to the open court.
    Tip #19: Never change the direction of an incoming crosscourt ball unless you can hurt your opponent.
    Tip #20: Tell your opponent when he is playing great.
    Tip #21: Hit the ball higher over the net than your opponent's last shot.
    Tip #22: Take a bathroom break and regroup if you lose a set quickly.
    Tip #23: Hit slice serves with new balls.
    Tip #24: Angle only if it's a winner.
    Tip #25: Drop shot only if you can afford to lose the point.
    Tip #26: Always take the full 90 seconds on a changeover.
    Tip #27: Never play a loose fifth point.
    Tip #28: Hit a second serve first if you miss three first serves in a row.
    Tip #29: Learn when to go for an ace.
    Tip #30: Realize that 30-love is overrated.
    Tip #31: Restart the point by centering the ball.

Tip #32: Learn the "twice, not once" theory of passing and volleying.

Tip #33: Never stand in the same place twice if you're up against a huge server.

Tip #34: Intimidate with consistency, not power, if your opponent is a weak server.

Tip #35: Retrieve a fresh grip and shirt if you've thought about it once.

Tip #36: Know the six steps to serving out a match.

Tip #37: Accept code violations.

Tip #38: Focus by controlling your eyes on the court in between points.

Tip #39: Stop thinking and start reacting (doubles vs. singles).

Tip #40: Know your game and play it on big points.

Tip #41: Always attack the middle.

Tip #42: Hit your first return up the line and then evaluate.

Tip #43: Use the double play (for the return and net player cross).

Tip #44: Keep moving; never just stand (net and return).

Tip #45: Position yourselves two-up or two-back.

Tip #46: Learn the three most important shots: first serve, first return, and first volley.

Tip #47: Use the "guts" poach (for returner's partner).

Tip #48: Hit at your opponent's right hip on a put away (left hip for a lefty).

Tip #49: Know and utilize formations.

Tip #50: Compliment your partner; never criticize after a bad play.

Tip #51: Laugh on changeovers.

Tip #52: Touch and talk after every point.

Tip #53: Wear something similar.

Tip #54: Take the middle ball when you're the player closest to the net.

Tip #55: Use the "Calkins play" on the second serve.

Tip #56: Learn "Graydon's play."

Tip #57: Isolate the weaker opponent.

Tip #58: Play "one bounce" doubles.

Tip #59: Practice after a loss to immediately feel better.

Tip #60: Build on victories.

Tip #61: Stop talking about your losses/loss to other players.

Tip #62: Take three things from each loss.

Tip #63: Accept losing.

Tip #64: Define class and make sure that you lose with it.

Tip #65: Eat something salty within 20 minutes after your match.

Tip #66: Watch how rarely the pros miss in the net.

Tip #67: Change your tension when all else fails.

Tip #68: Practice your overhead.

Tip #69: "Catch" the ball to improve volleys.

Introduction

Unless you are embedded deep in the tennis world, you have no idea who I am. You have never watched me play on TV. You've never seen me win a grand slam. I don't have an agent. There isn't a racket named after me. Pete Sampras doesn't have me on speed dial. So, why should you read this book?

Great question. The answer is, I am a damn good tennis player. I am ranked in the world. I have won a few minor league professional tournaments, called futures. (Baseball has the minor leagues and tennis has something very similar—highly competitive "futures," "satellites," and "challenger" circuits.) I have played tennis for most of my life. I learned to play hitting against the garage as a child. I'd play with my parents and older siblings until I could no longer stand up from exhaustion. I went from playing "knock out" at the local Racket Club with kids twice my age to winning the state tournament, being the best player in the Midwest, and receiving a college scholarship on a #1 NCAA-ranked and Big Ten championship team, the University of Illinois, to traveling the world as a professional tennis player. It's been quite a journey, and I've learned a lot.

I started to write this book in November 2003, while in Mexico playing a $10,000 tournament. I was in my second consecutive singles quarterfinal and doubles semifinal. Playing some good tennis, I didn't want to lose my form in the off-season. So I sat down one night and wrote a list of what I was doing particularly well—things off the court and on, before the match and after, in singles and doubles. Everything was originally written for me. Later, reading my notes, I thought: "These tips won't just help me, they will help every tennis player!"

This book includes tips I learned from other coaches I have met throughout my two decades of competitive tennis, and from other talented players. Many simply come from what I've learned on my own, through hard-won experience. All of them will help you. I know because all of them have helped me.

I certainly recommend reading the entire book start to finish. But reading any one of the tips can help you improve your tennis right now. Flip to any page, quickly read, and then go out and kick some butt!

1

Pre-Match

Tip #1: Stencil your rackets.

Tip #2: Look nice for matches.

Tip #3: Know your mental balance.

Tip #4: Do the "belly button" test.

Tip #5: Prepare on-court food and drink.

Tip #6: Serve out your match the night before.

Tip #7: Shoot free throws like Michael Jordan.

Tip #8: Include protein in your breakfast.

Tip #9: Learn nasal breathing and the sun salutation.

When I was in college, I learned how to cram for exams. In tennis, however, no such thing as cramming the night before a match exists. You can't make up for lost or wasted time by practicing eight hours straight the day before a tournament. You have to be working on your game every day.

The time before your match is hugely important. This chapter presents 10 ways to assure that you are ready to win your match. You have to be properly warmed up, be in the right mental state, and have your equipment and body 100 percent ready to go. Otherwise, you are setting yourself up for failure. Take it from me. I have learned some of these lessons the hard way. Nothing will make up for lack of preparation.

Tip #1: Stencil your rackets.

You've all seen the best player at your club or in the tournament. Word quickly spreads, with rumors about results and sponsors. "Bill gets Prince rackets for free," someone says. "I know because they make him stencil his rackets." Well, Bill's first-round match is already won before he even steps on the court. Yet any player can easily stencil his racket. The effect is incalculable.

Have you ever watched a pro tennis match on TV and seen a player without a stencil? Probably not. If you want to play to the height of your ability, then prepare your mind, body, and equipment like the pros. By using a stencil, you are communicating to yourself and your opponent that your racket and your game are pro caliber.

Stenciling your racket is easy. You just need the stencil logo of your racket company and the company's ink color (most companies use black, with the exception of Wilson), both of which can be purchased at virtually any tennis store. If you are winning the local tournament or your picture appears in the paper, contact your racket company's local representative and ask for a free stencil and ink. "Look," you should tell them, "I am giving your company tons of free advertising every time I step on the court." Racket companies love to see their logo on rackets, so they'll listen, even if you are just playing a small tournament.

These days, I get free rackets and products from Prince, but that wasn't always the case. I used to buy all my rackets and string, yet my competitors didn't know that information. Players just assumed that I received free products from Prince, and that assumption gave me an advantage, since only really good players get free stuff. Your competitors can't help but think you're better than they are before you've even stepped on the court.

Every top athlete talks of "attention to detail." Well, stenciling your racket is one small detail that can make a big difference.

Donald Miralle/Getty Images

Stenciling your racket is easy to do and will help you look like a professional.

Tip #2: Look nice for matches.

Unfortunately, clothing companies are not as flattered when they see their clothes on players as a racket company is when they see their stencil, but this advice has more to do with you than it does with getting wardrobe perks. The way you look on the court reveals the type of competitor you are. For instance, if a guy walks onto the court with two different colored socks, a half-ripped t-shirt, a scruffy beard, and a pair of old shoes, what is your impression? What if he walks onto the court looking sharp, wearing matching clothes with a colored shirt, and carrying a proper tennis bag? The difference is huge. Immediately, you treat your opponent as a solid player. Plenty of good players look terrible on court; however, they have to earn my respect before I give it to them. If my opponent looks like he has taken time to prepare his clothes, I expect he has also taken the time to prepare his body for a hard three-set match.

You might think this suggestion is shallow or prissy. Remember, football players don't walk onto the field with a helmet half painted and their shirts hanging out untucked. Team sports have equipment managers and rules that govern how they look. In tennis, you have to do it yourself. If you take the trouble to dress like a pro, you'll be that much closer to playing like one.

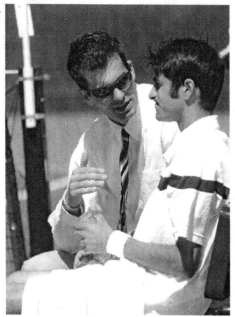

Wolverine Photo/Amir Gamzu

As a coach, dressing nicely for your players' matches communicates that their match is important to you. As a player, it communicates professionalism to yourself and your opponent.

Tip #3: Know your mental balance.

Do you listen to heavy metal or easygoing music? When you picture your ideal state of mind on the court, do you see an animal hunting its prey with ruthless intensity? Or do you play your best as a laid-back, chilled-out, happy-go-lucky dude who enjoys every moment?

Both of these types of players can be successful. However, you have to know what type you are and then make sure to arrive at that mental state before your match. Your body will only perform as well as your mind is prepared.

Ten minutes before my matches I always make sure to walk away from everyone. I like to listen to energetic music but also relax and stretch calmly by myself: breathing deeply, and taking care of my mental side (calm and collected) and physical side (loose and lightly sweating) before competing.

What is your ideal balance? What is the best way to find it? Only you can answer that question. A coach or parent can help, but only you can get yourself balanced.

Harry How/Getty Images

This player is intense but relaxed. What is your perfect mental balance?

My brother took forever to warm up, so he'd literally play an entire set before his match: a "warm-up" set. I know a player who would sit in a pitch-black room and meditate for 30 minutes before match time. Although completely different, both these players were successful at finding the right competitive balance.

Most club players and juniors have no idea what their ideal state of mind is. Think back to the last time that you truly played great tennis, when everything clicked, a day when you were competing hard for every point, putting all your returns in play, and playing to your potential. What was going through your head? Were you pumped or calm? Were you racing around between points or walking slowly? Are you a Bjorn Borg or a Jimmy Connors?

The best way to get into your ideal state is to make time alone before you compete. You won't always know when your match will start. Still, try to find at least 10 minutes when you can go somewhere alone and get into the proper mental state. Use music, meditation, exercise, or reading to help guide you to where you want to be. Finding the right internal balance before a match is as important as having your rackets strung and shoes tied.

Tip #4: Do the "belly button" test.

In warm-ups, aim your shot at your opponent's belly button and watch closely. It looks like you're just warming up, but really you are learning valuable information that will pay off when the match gets tight. When the ball was approaching your opponent's belly button, did he move around his backhand to hit a forehand, or around his forehand to hit a backhand? His reaction is a telltale sign that your opponent prefers one side to the other. Players run around their weaker side in warm-up because they're nervous and afraid of signaling that they have a terrible forehand or backhand. If it is so bad that they won't even hit it in warm-up, then make sure they have to hit it in the match.

Don't immediately play your opponent's "weaker" side. Instead, play your normal game, but at deuce points, for example, make sure that you make your opponent play the shot that he least prefers. Don't expect your opponent to miss; if he's a competent player, he should be able to make lots of balls from either wing. You can, however, expect a weaker ball.

Many players can't even identify their opponent's weaker side after a match. Use the first five minutes of the warm-up to find out this information immediately.

Tip #5: Prepare on-court food and drink.

Once you step onto the court and begin your match, you are unable to leave the court for any reason except to use the bathroom. So you have to make sure that anything you'll possibly need is already prepared and in your bag. I suggest preparing your bag well before you get to the courts. Once you're at the tournament site, you only want to be focused on your match.

So many myths exist about what to eat while competing. When you are on the court, you don't need protein. You need energy in the form of sugar. You are looking for a quick burst of energy that will sustain you through the match. Therefore, you should eat any type of food that is high on the glycemic index. (Finally, a time when it is okay to eat sugars!) Good choices include straight sugar, glucose, honey, white bread, ready-to-eat cereal, and pretzels. Skittles also work great. Some players eat fruit, peanut butter, or even sandwiches. These foods are good if it's early in the first set, but if you are looking for a quick burst of energy to finish off the match, your body does not have the proper amount of time to digest and glean energy from those foods. In between sets, grab a handful of Skittles even if you aren't hungry. The energy will help you replenish what you already lost playing the first set and will propel you into the second set.

While playing at the University of Illinois, we faced the challenge of playing southern teams in the NCAA tournament. The NCAA is always played in warm and humid conditions that our suntanned competitors were more prepared for. We played indoors for most of the winter and early spring. Outdoors, the points last longer, which means that fitness and dehydration play a much bigger role in preparing the body for peak performance. This situation is where sodium comes in. If you have ever had cramps, during or after a match, you know how debilitating they can be. Often, you'll be unable to continue playing. The absolute best cure for cramps is ingesting extra sodium—not salt pills or potassium (another myth about eating bananas), but a teaspoon of salt mixed with water or Gatorade. It might not taste the best, but it works. Make sure to prepare the mix before you step on the court, so it's ready to go right when you need it.

Have an on-court drink ready to go before your match so you can have it while competing.

Tip #6: Serve out your match the night before.

Picture an Olympic downhill skier minutes before his run. He's all alone on top of the mountain with his eyes closed, going through the course in his mind, his body turning and bobbing just as if he were doing it live. Would skiers do this exercise if it didn't help their chances of performing to the best of their ability? No.

So why aren't you practicing it? The night before all my matches, I find a place where I can be alone. I close my eyes and go through the motions, just like a skier, and I visualize all the emotions that I'll be feeling as well as the likely playing conditions. I may have blinding sun on my side, maybe my opponent will stall or use gamesmanship to try to throw me off my game, or maybe he'll be playing unbelievable tennis. Whatever the case may be, I rehearse the situation in my head, moving around and reacting. I practice my confident walk between points, my deep breathing, and the movement of my eyes. I practice all the important things that are found in the six steps to serving out a match (Tip #36). The next day, I think, "This is easy, I just did this."

Do you think your opponent has done the same exercise? I doubt it. You've done more to prepare before the match and it didn't require hours on the practice court or months of weight lifting. The biggest difference between a good player and a great player is his mental strength. Visualization is a way to improve and master that mental part of the game.

The biggest difficulty is finding a proper place to practice your visualization. If the tournament courts are busy, you will have to be creative: hotel banquet rooms, basements, parking lots, locker rooms, and beaches are places where I have found myself "serving out my match." Wherever you practice your visualization, make it as realistic as possible. I'll go through each motion that I would on the tennis court, but moving in slow motion. I'll hit my serve, recover for a forehand, run forward to the short ball, and play a volley and overhead to finish the point.

In the end, any competition comes down to who can mentally keep it together longer. Just as a dress rehearsal makes actors in a play more confident for the actual performances, serving out your match the night before will make you more confident while performing in the actual match. You've worked out the kinks beforehand. Also, you've convinced yourself that you will be serving out the match. By the time you've stepped on the court, you've already won.

Tip #7: Shoot free throws like Michael Jordan.

What sets great athletes apart from merely good athletes is inner confidence. Consider Michael Jordan: he radiated confidence. Jordan seemed to have no doubts about himself or his abilities. You could see his confidence when he was shooting free throws, standing all alone, chewing gum so confidently, with the game tied, millions of viewers watching, and all his teammates intensely staring…

Wouldn't it be great to play tennis with that kind of confidence? To get to that level, I always stand in front of a mirror for a quick 15 seconds before a match. I close my eyes and imagine that I am Jordan on the free throw line. When I feel as if I also radiate confidence, I open my eyes and look in the mirror. Then I take that vision, that look, onto the court and I am ready to battle.

This tactic might seem foolish, but I wouldn't recommend it if I didn't think it would make a big difference in your game. It's a great comfort to see that confidence staring back at you in the mirror. You might have experienced times on the court where you felt full of confidence, but what did it look like? Practice this exercise and you'll know.

Wolverine Photo/Amir Gamzu

The look in your eye translates into your on-court confidence.

Tip #8: Include protein in your breakfast.

It's uncommon to find a hotel that doesn't offer some sort of free breakfast. Tennis players check in for the tournament and think, "Great! Free breakfast." Wrong. Hotel breakfasts consist of nothing but cereals, bagels, toast, and waffles. Carbohydrates are important, and you should make sure to load up on them, but also make sure you're eating enough protein. For high-level tennis players, it's recommended that 10 to 20 percent of your diet should consist of protein. Three bowls of cereal from the continental breakfast might fill you up, but you'll need some protein to help your body recover and perform properly during your match.

Eggs are a great source of protein. The morning of a match, I try to consume about 15 grams of protein, along with my standard carbs (one large egg contains six grams of protein, so a breakfast of three eggs and toast will give you about 18 grams). Cheeses, yogurt, and nuts can also provide adequate protein.

When traveling, it can be expensive eating every breakfast in restaurants. However, it's worth it to do so. Eating a balanced breakfast with an adequate amount of protein will pay off during a tournament. A free breakfast consisting of sugar cereal will not cut it.

Filled up with Cocoa Puffs, your opponent will be out of energy by the third set. Meanwhile, you'll be doing cartwheels on changeovers.

Tip #9: Learn nasal breathing and the sun salutation.

Since the purpose of yoga is to coordinate the mind and the body, its tennis benefits are obvious. You hear of people working 80-hour weeks and then injuring themselves working out. You also hear of extremely talented athletes who are complete physical specimens, yet they can't perform mentally. In both cases, the body and the mind are on different pages.

By practicing deep nasal breathing and learning the sun salutation pose as discussed in John Douillard's book *Body, Mind, and Sport*, I immediately found my optimum mental state: an alert and focused "calmness." I had always been a "no pain, no gain" kind of guy. However, after practicing these two exercises just once, I felt like I had been given a gift. My brain was clear, and I felt free on the court. I was enjoying myself. I no longer yelled at my opponent, the umpires, or myself. I was playing tennis for fun and I was playing great. Give it a try. You don't have to become a practicing yogi. Just become familiar with this basic popular pose and method of breathing.

2

Match Play: Singles

Tip #10: Introduce yourself to your opponent.

Tip #11: Wear two pairs of socks.

Tip #12: Accept the weather.

Tip #13: Take a 30-second regroup before starting a tiebreaker.

Tip #14: Never miss returns.

Tip #15: Serve into the body on big points.

Tip #16: Lob high when on the run.

Tip #17: Loosen your grip.

Tip #18: Hit low volleys behind your opponent and high volleys to the open court.

Tip #19: Never change the direction of an incoming crosscourt ball unless you can hurt your opponent.

Tip #20: Tell your opponent when he is playing great.

Tip #21: Hit the ball higher over the net than your opponent's last shot.

Tip #22: Take a bathroom break and regroup if you lose a set quickly.

Tip #23: Hit slice serves with new balls.

Tip #24: Angle only if it's a winner.

Tip #25: Drop shot only if you can afford to lose the point.

Tip #26: Always take the full 90 seconds on a changeover.

Tip #27: Never play a loose fifth point.

Tip #28: Hit a second serve first if you miss three first serves in a row.

Tip #29: Learn when to go for an ace.

Tip #30: Realize that 30-love is overrated.

Tip #31: Restart the point by centering the ball.

Tip #32: Learn the "twice, not once" theory of passing and volleying.

Tip #33: Never stand in the same place twice if you're up against a huge server.

Tip #34: Intimidate with consistency, not power, if your opponent is a weak server.

Tip #35: Retrieve a fresh grip and shirt if you've thought about it once.

Tip #36: Know the six steps to serving out a match.

Tip #37: Accept code violations.

Tip #38: Focus by controlling your eyes on the court in between points.

Tip #39: Stop thinking and start reacting (doubles vs. singles).

Tip #40: Know your game and play it on big points.

Singles tennis is a difficult game. You're all alone on the court and everything is up to you. No better feeling exists than sitting down after a singles win and letting the satisfaction take over your entire body. You won because of you. It's a very addictive feeling, and you can feed that addiction by taking your time to master these tips.

The 31 tips in this chapter are specifically on-court singles tactics and strategies. I'm giving you many tips because many ways exist to win a tennis match. Any coach that says otherwise needs to start looking for a new job. Plus, you'll actually be able to follow these tips. I am not telling you to hit winners on every point, nor am I recommending that you change your style of play. The game that you have right now is good enough to win—if you take my advice.

Should the tips be written in stone? Absolutely! At the same time, you don't want zillions of thoughts racing through your head after each point. What's most important is keeping a clear and positive attitude. It'll take time for the tips to soak in. For example, Tip #18 discusses where to hit your volley ("Hit low volleys behind your opponent and high volleys to the open court"). Just reading that tip is not going to make you a wonderful volleyer, but it will give you something to slowly incorporate into your practices and matches. As your volleying improves, move onto the next tip. Your game will improve by leaps and bounds if you don't rush the learning process.

Reading these tips, you might think that I'm taking all the fun out of tennis. Well, after practicing these techniques and maintaining a more disciplined game, I found myself playing the best tennis of my life. I didn't miss the cute stuff I'd given up. Once you start winning, as well as understanding why you are winning, you'll find no greater thrill.

Tip #10: Introduce yourself to your opponent.

What's the first thing that basketball players do before the jump ball? They all go around and slap hands and quickly chat. Sumo wrestlers bow to each other before competing. Tennis players don't have this kind of greeting. So, use that situation to your advantage. Introducing yourself to your opponent communicates something about yourself before you've even struck a ball.

First, it says that you don't have a chip on your shoulder. I have played qualifying matches without umpires, against players that were supposedly big cheats, and I had no problems at all, because I created an enjoyable and respectful competitive arena.

Second, introducing yourself says you're not afraid. Tennis players often psyche themselves out against a higher-ranked player before the match even begins. I have seen junior players that can't even make eye contact with the number one seed in the tournament because they're so intimidated. A great way to squash that intimidation is to walk over confidently, look your competitor in the eye, give him a nice firm handshake, and say, "Hi, I'm Michael, nice to meet you." (Don't say "Michael" if you have a different name; saying that name will only confuse things). Your opponent will feel your confidence before even playing one point.

Introducing yourself is also a matter of respect. Let's say your opponent is a weaker or inexperienced competitor who feels out of place. We've all felt that way. By introducing yourself, you're saying, "I don't care if you're the worst player in the world, I still respect you and your game, and because of that respect, I will give you no free points." You want your opponent to know that you compete hard and that you compete with class. If your opponent isn't close to being your equal, then get the job done and get out. Never blow off your opponent. If you greet your opponent, you will play better because you will have handled the situation with class, and your opponent will respect you.

Also, you never know, an opponent could be your next doubles partner. You find out a lot about an athlete in competition. Is this person someone you would want to play doubles with? Travel with? Train with? Tennis is an individual sport, so you have to rely on other players to practice and travel with. It helps if your opponent knows who you are.

In tennis, you play against all kinds of interesting people. Why not get to know your competitors? Wouldn't it be beneficial to know somebody living in L.A., New York, Australia, or England; or, to have access to people who are competitive, hard working, athletic, and driven? Companies pay millions of dollars a year to identify those people. You are meeting and competing with them every day, so use that knowledge to your advantage. Also, don't worry if your opponent won't shake your hand. I once had a

Korean player spit on my hand. That incident was a bit odd, but I immediately knew that I was dealing with a classless hothead. Needless to say, deep into the first set, my opponent erupted and I went on to win. Nice to meet you too!

Knowing who your opponents are is important for many reasons.

Tip #11: Wear two pairs of socks.

Take one look at any avid tennis players' feet and you'll never want to look again. Their feet are banged up, bruised, and discolored. Why? Tennis requires so much starting and stopping movements that our feet get destroyed in the process.

Tennis players have to find a way to take care of their feet, the most important part of their body. A lot of players have shoulder, back, and knee problems from playing, but nothing determines whether you can keep playing more than the health of your feet. I always wear two pairs of socks on the court, which gives me two times the cushioning and allows me to play longer and harder. Lleyton Hewitt wears three pairs of socks every time he steps on the court, so clearly he understands the benefits. Also, the more comfortable you feel on the court, the better your chances of competing like a pro. If you can afford a good pair of orthotics, get them; if not, even a generic cushion that fits in the sole of your shoe will cut back on all the pounding. Your feet will thank you.

Darrin Braybrook/ALLSPORT

Taking care of your feet is one of the most important things you can do.

Tip #12: Accept the weather.

News flash: *nobody likes playing in the wind!* From the highest level to the worst club player, poor weather bothers everybody. Extreme heat, freezing cold, bad lighting, rain, bright sun, you name it—weather is always a factor. I was once getting ready to serve and the wind blew over my chair on the side of the court. I received a code violation for "throwing my chair," even though I was standing 30 feet away from it.

Now, what can you do about the weather? Nothing. All you can do is accept it and move on. Stop being a baby and start competing like a winner. Remember the 2004 U.S. Open quarterfinal match between Roger Federer and Andre Agassi? It was one of the windiest matches in U.S. Open history, but both Federer and Agassi have the championship attitude that is needed to handle poor weather. In matches, the right response to bad weather is: "Okay, this weather is a test—a test that I'll pass by keeping my cool and focusing on the things that I can control. I know my opponent is unhappy with these conditions, so let's show him I am not bothered by them." You always see a few players in tournaments who don't complain about the weather and just accept the situation. Those are the players that are getting the most out of their game.

I'm not saying to go outside in 50 mile per hour winds and 40 degree temperatures when you have indoor courts available for practice. However, if you know you'll be competing in tough conditions, bad weather is a great practice opportunity. You learn how to deal with tough conditions and which shots work in bad weather.

So first, stop talking about it. Next, simplify your game plan. If it's 120 degrees on the court and 100 percent humidity, you might want to use a very aggressive game plan to shorten the points. If it's gusting, play the middle of the court and stay away from angles, therefore, minimizing the effect of the wind. Finally, laugh at it. After whiffing your overhead due to extreme sun, laugh out loud. Come on, it's funny.

If you blame the weather for your loss, you were bound to lose anyway. The weather is not the deciding factor in who wins a tennis match. Respond to the challenge of the conditions. Learn to do what the pros do: don't let weather bother you. You'll take your game and your mental toughness to a new level.

Accepting the weather is not always easy but always mandatory.

Tip #13: Take a 30-second regroup before starting a tiebreaker.

When a match reaches a tiebreaker, it goes without saying that you have two very evenly matched opponents competing. The question is, what will separate the winner from the loser? Breakers are commonly referred to as "busters" because that's exactly what a lot of players do: they bust, or break, under the pressure. Whatever happened earlier in the match no longer matters. It doesn't matter how many great shots you hit or aces you smashed. It all comes down to the tiebreaker. Kind of scary, isn't it? However, tiebreakers are also the best part of playing tennis because they test your confidence and your ability to handle pressure.

Before the breaker, you need to take a 30-second time-out so to speak, much like a football team will before overtime. Since we don't have a bench of teammates or on-court coaches in tennis, come crunch time, you have to find ways to refocus on your own. I always take my time walking around the court before a tiebreaker. I stand near the back of the court and focus my eyes on my strings. I divide my 30-second time-out into two sections, each one 15 seconds long. During the first 15 seconds, I have one thought: "I love tie-breakers. I love coming up big when it matters the most." Convince yourself of this statement. Say it out loud.

Use the next 15 seconds to develop a simple but effective strategy. Ask yourself this question: how am I going to win points in this breaker? I hate to over-think on the court. Remember to KISS: Keep It Simple Stupid. Are you going to attack the net? Are you going to play back on the baseline and let your opponent dictate? Are you going to approach his forehand? Whatever has been working for you during the match should still be your strategy. Just condense and simplify your game plan.

Too many players immediately rush into the tiebreaker, and by the time they have found their composure and winning strategy, they are down 3-0, 4-1, or 5-2. At this point, the set is as good as over. If you use this tip, those problems might exist for your opponent, but not for you.

Phil Cole/Getty Images

Looking at your strings is a great way to regroup between points.

Tip #14: Never miss returns.

As you move up the competitive ladder, you'll find that the better the player, the less he gives away. You can see evidence of this principle at your own club. Who's the best player at your club? Go watch him play a match and count how many returns he gets in play. Then count how many returns you make in a match. I bet you'll see a significant difference. Even if your returns are weak or slow, if you're getting them in, your opponent will understand that he'll have to work to earn every point.

Accomplished players make their opponents work. You can't just have a huge serve. At some point, you'll have to break serve if you want to win. People criticize Andy Roddick, Pete Sampras, and others for having huge serves and nothing else. However, they rarely miss any returns. It's true they almost never hit winners, but they get the ball into the court. Over the course of a match, they will get their chances. You can do the same, but how?

The best thing to do is practice. Don't neglect the second most important shot in the game by not practicing the return. To groove your return, have your practice partner serve 50 balls to the deuce court and 50 to the ad court, and keep track of how many you hit successfully. Unless you're playing against a serve-and-volleyer, you have no reason to miss the return in the net. Lob the return if you have to. Clear the net, and get that ball in the court. If you were able to get your racket on the ball, then you had to be able to get the ball over the net.

Wolverine Photo/Amir Gamzu

Staying low and looking ready will translate into many great returns.

It's okay to chip returns. I used to play tennis with a guy that would say, "Chips are for parties, not for returning," but watch the pros. They all chip returns just to get the serve back and the point started. You might think it's wimpy, but not when your opponent starts missing them. Think of the chip return as a volley. Using the same grip, get the racket out in front of you, and volley the ball into the middle of the court. You will be amazed at how many more points you'll win just because you got the return in play. If your opponent starts to move forward or hit winners off your soft returns, then you might have to adjust your game plan. However, see if he can do it at 5-5.

Don't prepare to return serve by standing still. Get moving. Bounce on your feet, shuffle, or stutter step. Your opponent will feel your presence and know that nothing's getting past you. Also, it's a lot easier to make those necessary minor adjustments if you're already moving.

Obviously, missing returns is never anyone's goal. However, this tip simply says to get the ball back, one way or another. It doesn't matter how it looks; you don't receive extra points for beauty. Once you become a wall and get everything back in play, your opponent will quickly lose his serve. An uptight and worried server makes a lot less of his first serves. With more second serves, you can become more aggressive.

Clive Brunskill/Getty Images

Get the serve back and in play, one way or another.

Tip #15: Serve into the body on big points.

The average club player has four placements of the serve: out wide and up the "T" on both the deuce court and the ad court. However, the most effective and least common serve is the body serve.

Faced with a body serve, your opponent has to decide what stroke to use, forehand or backhand. This decision requires quick thinking and quick moving. Every player has a side he prefers. I prefer to return with my backhand, since my swing is more compact and powerful; but, if you serve to my body, I'll have to make a lot of calculations and adjustments to play to my strength. If you serve to either of my "wings," I have no choices and very few calculations to make. You've only simplified things for me because my return involves very little thinking and very little complication.

The beauty of the body serve is that you can serve them up all day and they'll still work. If it's 30-30 or deuce and the game score is tied, I am serving into the body 90 percent of the time. Even if my opponent knows this strategy ahead of time, what can he do about it? Move over a little? Stand farther back? Okay, but then I can take advantage with my other serves.

Let's be honest. On big points, things don't always go as planned. The arm tightens up and the legs get a little wobbly. Make things easy for yourself and serve into the body to give yourself plenty of margin for error. If you're serving up the "T" or out wide, you can only miss one way and still have the ball go in. Serving into the body, you can miss either left or right, and your serve is still in the box. You just doubled your chances of making a first serve on a big point. This advantage is huge.

The next time you hit serves, put three targets in each box instead of two: out wide, in the body, and down the "T." Now, you have a total of six serves in your bag of tricks instead of four. I just increased your serving repertoire by 33 percent. Those extra serves are a big difference and one that your opponent will notice. A slice serve works best, but if you can't hit one, simply picture a target on your opponent's chest and aim. While he's fumbling around, you can step up and take advantage of the weak return. On big points, stick to percentages and hurt your opponent, literally and figuratively, with a body serve.

Big point? Go with a body serve.

Tip #16: Lob high when on the run.

If you ever get the chance to watch live, pro tennis, bring a notebook. One thing you'll note is when the world's best players are stretched out, they throw a defensive lob up that nearly touches the moon.

When your opponent has you on the run and you can barely get your racket on the ball, do your best to send that lob extremely high. The higher the lob, the harder it is to hit the overhead. Your opponent can only do two things: try to calculate the speed and height and hit it in the air, or let the ball bounce. Either way, you're in better shape than if you simply sent him an easy put-away. For one thing, you've given yourself time to get back in the point. Throw that lob sky-high, get back to the middle of the court, and get your racket and feet ready for the overhead.

You might remember that famous point Jimmy Connors played against the Dutch player Paul Haarhuis in the 1991 U.S. Open quarterfinal. Connors was throwing balls up high into the night sky, and eventually, he got his chance to hurt his opponent by hitting a running backhand passing shot winner. Connors went on to win the match in four sets.

Never give your opponent an easy overhead. Make him earn the point. If you get the ball high enough and deep enough, your opponent might opt to play a forehand or backhand instead of an overhead. When your opponent doesn't hit an overhead, you have successfully restarted the point.

Wolverine Photo/Amir Gamzu

This lob will be high and difficult for the opponent.

Tip #17: Loosen your grip.

"Tighter is not better," one of my childhood coaches would always tell me. It really is great advice. It's very important to stay loose while competing. From professional tennis to professional basketball, it is very common to see athletes smiling or laughing while they are competing. This action is nothing but a trick that helps the athlete relax, take some pressure off, and enjoy the moment.

An easy way to tell if you are already relaxed while on the tennis court is to evaluate how tight you are holding onto the racket. Do not choke the racket handle to death. Yet, the majority of club players will grip the racket as if they were suffocating it. Why? The only time that you need to slightly tighten your grip is right before you make contact with the ball, and trust me, your body will automatically react for you. If it didn't, the racket would fly out of your hand every time you hit.

When you hold the racket too tightly, the hitting arm starts to wear itself out and get tired. It is equivalent to flexing the forearm muscle for as long as you are on the court. Instead, try this: during a point and in between shots, spin the racket in your hand. This action will require you to loosen up that grip. If you are holding too tight, it will be impossible to spin the racket. Next time you get a chance to watch top level tennis, take a look at the player who is not hitting the ball. You will find that he is either spinning the racket or loosening his grip as he prepares for his next shot. You should do the same.

A loose grip equals a loose hitting arm, which equals a loose body and torso. Start each shot the absolute right way by relaxing that hand. You'll be surprised at how much better you hit the ball.

Wolverine Photo/Amir Gamzu

Relax your grip on the racket in between
(and during) points to keep your arm loose.

Tip #18: Hit low volleys behind your opponent and high volleys to the open court.

Most tennis players are afraid of the net. They treat the net as if flesh-eating sharks are surrounding it. In public park tennis or USTA league matches, players only go to the net to pick up the balls and shake hands. At higher levels, even baseliners know they'll have to come in to the net to finish points.

In most cases, the volley is the last shot players learn. You first learn the forehand and backhand, then the serve, and possibly the overhead. I didn't learn how to hit proper volleys until I got to college.

In junior tennis, players can win just staying on the baseline. Juniors who do serve and volley lose early, often, and start to doubt their games. However, they are on the right track. It'll pay off down the road, while the kids who stayed on the baseline are finding the net game very difficult to play. As a junior player, I stayed on the baseline, grinding away my matches like everybody else. When I got to college, I had to take a step back and develop a net game. I can only imagine where I'd be now if at 13 years old I stopped worrying about my sectional or national boys' 14 and under ranking and instead learned how to play the net. Instead of writing this book, I'd be on TV winning grand slams.

You have no reason to be scared of the net. The first thing to understand about net play is that you don't have to win the point with your first volley. The more volleys you put in the court, the more you are forcing your opponent to go for an impossible passing shot. Pressure is a funny thing, and when your opponent is trying to pass you, he's feeling a lot of it.

Very little guesswork is associated with smart net play. Coming into the net, you're faced with two options: a low volley or a high volley. For low volleys, go behind the opponent. For high volleys, go into the open court.

I know it sounds simplistic, but simplicity is the point. To improve your game, we have to simplify. Too many players take low volleys or half volleys and try to play them into the open court. By placing the low volley back down the line, you are making your job easier. For one thing, you aren't changing the direction of the ball (if your opponent hits to you down the line, then you volley back down the line; if he hits to you crosscourt, then volley crosscourt). Play difficult volleys safely, saving the aggressive play for an easier, high volley. You've taken your opponent's great shot and said, "Okay, now do it again." Usually when this occurs, you get your high volley. You are also forcing your opponent to make difficult adjustments. A ball hit directly to a player requires the player to adjust with small steps while being balanced enough to still make a play on the ball. Players have an easier time running down shots in the open court than adjusting to a ball that is jamming into their body.

Keep in mind, the definition of a low volley and high volley is not what the trajectory of the ball is. It is defined as what height the ball is at when you are hitting it. If your opponent pops up a soft ball, but you are slow to react and end up hitting it below the level of the net, then it's a low volley.

High volleys should be hit into the open court for this simple reason: it is easier to be aggressive with high volleys. You can stick a high volley into the open court and watch your opponent run. You have less risk in changing the direction of the ball and more of an opportunity to end the point. Besides, if you're coming into net, you are already halfway to an aggressive play, so you might as well finish the job. Seems easy right? Well, it is.

Wolverine Photo/Amir Gamzu

A high volley is your opportunity to hurt your opponent.

Tip #19: Never change the direction of an incoming crosscourt ball unless you can hurt your opponent.

After watching players on TV hit the ball crosscourt to each other over and over again, my mom always says, "Why don't they just hit it to the open court?" It's a good question. It seems like the players aren't doing anything to win the point; they're just hitting back and forth. However, they don't hit it to the open court because they're waiting to hurt their opponent with the right ball.

I once worked with a coach that made me name 15 reasons to never change the direction of an incoming crosscourt ball. A bit over the top, but his point was that I'd better be real sure it's the right time to hit up the line or else I'd get burned. Think about it, you have a lot to lose and little to gain. First, the net is shorter when hitting crosscourt (three feet at center strap) as opposed to down the line (three feet six inches at the end of the net). Second, you're working with much more distance (82.5 feet from corner to corner versus 78 feet down the line). Third, it's easier to keep the direction of the ball the same; that is, if you hit back crosscourt, your swing matches the incoming path of the ball. Fourth, if you haven't hit a winner up the line, you've left an open court that your opponent can easily attack by hitting crosscourt (the highest percentage shot).

By playing the ball back crosscourt over and over again, you're telling your opponent, "I am going to hit back and forth all day until I get a ball that I can hurt you with." When you do get the right ball, such as a short ball or a ball that you know you can be aggressive with, then by all means, rip it down the line. You deserve it because you just played 10 balls crosscourt. Give yourself a lot of room for error and aim for a spot in the middle of no man's land, but swing aggressively; otherwise, you'll just find yourself in another crosscourt battle, only this time, it will be on the backhand side.

Don't get me wrong, I'm not saying you should never hit down the line. When you do, you need to be 100 percent sure it is the right play.

Clive Brunskill/Getty Images

Based on court position, this shot should be played back crosscourt to minimize risk.

Tip #20: Tell your opponent when he is playing great.

Some of the best athletes in the world use rule-bending tricks like this one to help them win. Let's say you're getting killed and your opponent is in the zone. He's hitting lines left and right, serving aces, and ripping return winners. It happens to everybody at every level. A guy that you normally beat is destroying you.

When your opponent is controlling, and you feel like you're losing control of the match, you might try playing moon balls, taking extra time between points, using the bathroom, standing farther in to return, etc. However, I don't think it hurts to also tell your opponent he's zoning. In fact, it usually helps.

Seeded number two in a qualifying match in Montreal, I was losing to an unknown player 7-5, 4-2. I knew that I was better than him, but it was his day. I hadn't seen his second serve yet and I couldn't get close to breaking him. At 4-2, as we were

Don't be afraid to speak to your opponent; sometimes, it will make all the difference.

Wolverine Photo/Amir Gamzu

exchanging balls at the net, I said, "Wow, you are serving great, you've made 27 first serves in a row." He didn't say much; in fact, I don't think he even knew it. When you're in the zone, you aren't thinking. Suddenly though, he double-faulted twice and I broke him primarily off his second serves. I went on to win the match.

I won because I changed his focus. I got him out of his zone. He went from being instinctive and relaxed to analytical and uptight. It wasn't against the rules. I wasn't cheating him or being a jerk. I was simply trying to get him back down to planet Earth, and it worked.

I've heard a story about Vic Braden losing to Bobby Riggs with his best shot, which was his backhand. At the changeover, Riggs said to Braden, "Don't worry Vic, your backhand will come back, just keep working on it." Needless to say, Braden's backhand went to the toilet, and Riggs won the match.

Tennis is more mental than physical, so if your opponent is playing great tennis, do something within the rules to disrupt his mental game. Make him earn it. Get him thinking, but be clever and polite about it.

Tip #21: Hit the ball higher over the net than your opponent's last shot.

They say that speed kills, but so does depth. We've all played somebody who doesn't hit the ball that hard or heavy, but he hits it deep. How can you hurt somebody if he's constantly pushing you back with his depth? You can't, which is why depth is so important. Coaches are always saying, "Deeper, deeper, deeper," but how do you accomplish that depth?

Instead of focusing on where the ball lands, focus on the height of the ball as it crosses the net. Instead of, "deeper, deeper, deeper," tell yourself, "higher, higher, higher."

While warming up and early on in the match, I gauge my net clearance off of my opponent. If his incoming ball is two feet over the net, then I make mine clear the net by three feet. You can also do this exercise while practicing by yourself or with a coach. Every time your shot crosses the net, shout, "Yes!" if your shot is higher than your opponent's or shout, "No!" if it isn't. The goal is to get in the habit of consistently hitting the ball higher over the net than your opponent's last shot.

Tip #22: Take a bathroom break and regroup if you lose a set quickly.

Some days when everything should be going right, nothing does. You warm up, stretch, and are all ready to go, and then *boom*, 10 minutes into your match, you lose the first set 6-0. When I find myself in this situation, I always take a bathroom break. Every league and governing body has its own rules, but you should always be able to take a bathroom break no matter where you play.

Obviously, the importance of this break is not to actually use the bathroom (although, after losing a set in that way, you might have to), but to take more time than the 90 seconds allowed on a changeover. However much time you have, make sure you use all of it. Most governing bodies allow a 'reasonable time,' but some allow no more than three minutes, so make sure you know the rules. You are taking this break to slow things down for not only yourself, but also your opponent. During the break, analyze what went wrong and what needs to be done to fix it.

First, don't panic. A two out of three set match is a race to two, and you are only down 1-0. The score is not important. What matters is how you play the next set. Losing sets, just like losing points, is part of the game. Just because this set was quick doesn't mean the entire match will be. By taking a break, you are already doing the right thing, which is making smart decisions. Draw confidence from those decisions.

Second, ditch your game plan and go to your money shots. Obviously, your initial game plan didn't work. Toss it away and go to what you do best. Go to the part of your game that has won matches in the past. See if your opponent can handle your weapons.

Third, think about the present. After losing a bad set, it's easy to start thinking about the future or the past, but don't. Be mentally disciplined. The set is over and you can't change it. Bring yourself back to the present moment, one point at a time. That focus will keep you competing hard, no matter what the score. Before you know it, you've clawed your way back into the match.

Finally, focus on that first game after taking the break. You have to immediately show your opponent that you are still in this match. Your opponent is probably thinking it's going to be an easy match, so prove him wrong.

Losing a quick set can be a wake-up call, but only if you do the right things to wake up. Losing 6-0 is no worse than losing in a tiebreaker. No matter how you slice it, it's just one set. You can still win this thing.

Tip #23: Hit slice serves with new balls.

On the ATP tour, balls are changed every seven and nine games. So, they change after the first seven games (for example, 4-3), and every nine games after (i.e., 6-4, 3-3). In the futures and satellites, which are run by the ITF, balls are changed every 11 and 13 games. With new balls, the big servers are at a huge advantage. Newer balls are noticeably faster for the first couple of games (until they get fluffed up again). Newer balls also grip the strings of the racket better, causing a more intense spin reaction.

A very good player I've played doubles with always hits a slice serve with new balls. It's a good tactic. Sliced hard, new balls will bounce very differently. Even if your opponent knows the slice is coming, he's not going to know how much the slice will affect a new ball. He hasn't gotten used to how the ball reacts to spins.

I know what you are thinking: "The matches I play don't get a change of balls." Well, okay, but almost every tournament in the nation offers new balls for the third set. That first game in the deciding set of a club or league match could be the turning point of the match. If you are serving first, you can immediately get some momentum by using the new balls to your advantage. Also, if a ball is somehow lost during the match, don't just decide to play with the remaining two. Instead, get a new ball and then slice the hell out of it. You are not cheating; in fact, you aren't even bending the rules.

I know a player who keeps one of the balls in his pocket for most of the match and uses the other balls for nearly all the points. Then, on a big point at 30-all or deuce, he'll unleash the fresh ball. "Nice serve," his opponents will say. More like, nice new ball. (You can prevent this serve from happening as a returner by always requesting all three balls when you serve).

By the way, a slice serve doesn't necessarily mean an out wide serve in the deuce court. You can use a slice serve in both boxes with many different targets. My absolute favorite serve is a slice in the deuce court that starts at the "T" and ends up in my opponent's body. In the ad court, you can slice a heavy serve up the "T" and watch the ball spin away from your opponent. Using this same spin in the ad court, you can slice to a right-hander's backhand side and spin the ball into the body. Either way, the biggest thing to remember with the slice is to hit a slice. You'll have the flat and kick serve when the balls fluff up.

You'll see it used on TV all the time. In pro tennis, it's considered sportsmanlike to show your opponent new balls before you serve. The players hold up the balls so the opponent knows they're fresh. Take advantage of the fact that amateur tennis doesn't observe the same etiquette. Get up to the line and slice that first serve. 15-love.

Tip #24: Angle only if it's a winner.

One of the first things my college coach told me after watching a high school match of mine was that I miss too many balls wide. "Do I?" I thought, "I have no idea." I had always thought an error was an error and it didn't matter whether it was wide, long, or in the net. However, I learned you have no reason to miss wide unless the shot was going to be a winner (and most of the shots I missed wide weren't going to be winners). You'll find the same is true of your game. Keep track of how many wide balls you miss in your next match, as well as how many would have been winners if you hadn't missed. You'll see that you are missing wide for no good reason.

"I want to get my opponent to move off the court," you're probably thinking, "I want to make him run." Fine, but if you aren't playing tour events (and no, the *Louisville Bob Evans Sausage and Biscuit Open* is not a tour event), you should stop playing the angles.

In addition to the high likelihood that you'll miss wide, remember that when you hit an angled shot, you are creating an equal angle of attack for your opponent. In other words, if you pull him way off the court, he can easily return the favor, particularly since he doesn't have to change the direction of the incoming ball. Also, if he's faster than you, forget about trying it. If you're the faster player, it might be worth a shot once in awhile. However, if your opponent is smart, he'll simply play the ball deep crosscourt (not changing direction) or up the middle of the court, and you will have to recreate another low percentage angle.

What constitutes an angle? I go by the two bounce rule. Hit a normal shot over the net and let the ball bounce twice. Where did the ball land on the second bounce? If you extended the two singles sidelines until they hit the back fence, did the second bounce land inside or outside of the imaginary box you've created? If it landed outside, consider it an angle. When you're hitting ground strokes, notice where your shots are landing and imagine where the second bounce would land. As you become more consistent hitting within this two bounce box, increase its size to the doubles sideline, giving yourself a bit more angle to work with. As you get even better, you can draw even wider imaginary lines.

"So you're asking me to only hit the ball up the middle?" No. I am saying to hit within the two-bounce rule box until you feel you can hurt your opponent. If you play the percentages, hitting the ball more or less up the middle of the court and over the lowest part of the net, you will eventually get a short and weak ball you can attack. This technique is a much simpler and more effective way to construct points.

If you choose to angle, make sure it's going to be a winner.

Tip #25: Drop shot only if you can afford to lose the point.

Why is it that the least talented try to hit the most drop shots? How many drop shots did you see at the U.S. Open this year? Almost none. How many drop shots did you see at last week's 2.5 USTA league match? A lot. Why? It's because weaker players are tired and need to end the point soon, and also because they delude themselves into thinking it will work. The first reason I understand. If you're tired, a drop shot can quickly turn a long rally into a short one—but one you usually lose.

It looks easy, a small little tap over the net and out of your opponent's reach. However, to successfully hit a drop shot, you need great touch, the right spin, and most importantly, your opponent needs to be in the right position. Usually, though, he's in better position than you think and can easily run the ball down for a simple put away.

I'll admit, it is a sweet feeling to hit a soft winner and watch your opponent run like hell and still not get to it. On the other hand, is that one success worth the 10 times it doesn't work?

I suppose a time and place for this slow but offensive shot does exist—if, say, your opponent stays very far back on the baseline, is very slow, or is just too tired to run a ball down. A drop shot in these instances could be a good play to keep your opponent honest. However, having been burned so many times by trying to be cute, I now only hit drop shots when I can afford to lose the point. Under those circumstances, I'm feeling less pressure and will likely hit a better shot. If it's a big point, you will be a bit tighter and chances are you won't execute the shot.

The best players in the world understand that the success rate is low, and to succeed in tennis you have to play the percentages. The better the player, the more patience he has to win long points. Indulge yourself only at 40-15 or 40-love—that is, when losing the point isn't the end of the world.

Tip #26: Always take the full 90 seconds on a changeover.

I understand most people reading this book aren't playing with chair umpires, but I still recommend you take 90 seconds each changeover, no matter what the score or how you're feeling at the time. Taking the full time is a way of pacing yourself, which, in turn, fosters consistency.

It surprises me how many players start walking to the other side of the court after quickly drying off with a towel and taking a sip of water. Take every second. You have the time to help you relax and rest. Most pros push the time limit a little, even if they're up a set and a break, thereby conserving energy for later in the match. You should do the same. Clock yourself on changeovers. If you're in better shape than your opponent, don't let the minute and a half stretch into two minutes. Call "time" as the pros do. It's not poor sportsmanship, it's the rule.

Even if my opponent has gotten up and is standing on the baseline ready to serve, I let him wait the full 90 seconds—sometimes more if it's a hot or humid day. Waiting isn't gamesmanship or superstition but a way to keep my body in the same rhythm on every changeover. The longer the match, the more important rhythm becomes, which means the more important your changeover is. Watch a great baseball pitcher at work. His rhythm and routine on the mound is crucial to his concentration. Taking 10 seconds one changeover, 60 seconds another, sometimes sitting down, sometimes standing up, drinking sometimes, other times talking to your opponent, etc.—all this inconsistency takes you out of your rhythm.

Whether you put a towel over your head at every changeover (as I do) or retie your shoes, you should stick to a routine that suits your temperament. Sit down and drink water, breathing deeply with your eyes controlled on the ground, or staring into space (not watching other courts or talking). Towel off. Inspect your equipment. Retie your shoes. Close your eyes and find a sense of calmness. Take another drink and then refocus on the next game.

Maybe you can't focus on calmness. Maybe you want to quickly analyze each point in the last two games. Maybe you have to change your shirt every three games because it's soaked with sweat. Maybe you want to keep your eyes open the whole time and stare at a tennis ball. Do whatever you want. I have seen players listen to music or pray, and a famous picture of Jim Courier showed him reading a book on a changeover (versus Andrei Medvedev at the 1993 ATP World Championship). Whole books could be written on what to do with your changeover. The key, however, is to develop a routine so you can find and maintain that inner balance before the next game. Are you the type of player who needs to be a ravenous animal on the court? If so, maybe you should listen to energetic music, keep your feet moving, or read something motivational during your changeover. If you have giant ups and giant downs on the court, it's likely that your changeovers aren't paced to keep you in a more stable state of mind.

Even if you play two terrible games, or get spooked by a bad call, you can immediately get it back by going through your changeover routine. Eventually, your changeover will become a conditioned response that forces you back into your perfect mental state for competition.

Robert Laberge/Getty Images

Your changeover routine is extremely important, so make sure you have a good one.

Tip #27: Never play a loose fifth point.

Three possible fifth points of a game are 30-all, 40-15, and 15-40. Each fifth point should be treated with special care. In both singles and doubles, you will be stunned at how many more return games you will win by winning the fifth point. Anyone that consistently plays fifth points with killer intensity gives his opponents nightmares.

In the event of the score being 30-all, you don't have to be Bud Collins to know how crucial it is. That occasion is where you go with your best shots and your highest percentage plays.

When you're down in the score, it's easy to check out and quickly lose the game. Being down 15-40 might seem like you are a long way from winning the game—in fact, you are. You're four consecutive points away. On the other hand, you're only two consecutive points away from tying the score, at which point your chances become as good as your opponent's at winning the game. Down 40-15, you'll often get a free point if you just play high percentage tennis. Maybe your opponent double faults or makes an unforced error. Before he knows it, he's kicking himself and feeling like the game has slipped away from him. Good. You've capitalized on his complacency and put yourself back into the game. By winning the fifth point, you start swinging the momentum back your way.

What if you're up 40-15? We've all done it. We start thinking about the next game. Recognizing the importance of the fifth point will help you focus and finish the game you're in now. Don't wait for 40-30. Get it done now. Who knows, maybe your opponent will hit a let-cord winner, or maybe a beautiful woman will sit down and distract you. You cannot relax. Say, "Fifth point," to yourself as a trigger to sharpen your concentration.

Phil Cole/Getty Images

Every shot is crucial on the fifth point.

Tip #28: Hit a second serve first if you miss three first serves in a row.

It always amazes me how many players go a whole game without making a first serve—four, 125 mile an hour first serves into the net. If you miss three first serves, hit your second serve and get it in play. You'll be learning from your mistakes and taking the pressure off your second serve. Returners will also be less aggressive, even if your serve comes over the net like a wounded duck.

You should never miss three first serves in a row. However, if you do, evaluate where you've been missing. If most are long, then you know your toss is too far behind your head. If they're in the net, you know to stay up and stand "taller" when making contact. Learning to recognize patterns in your errors isn't easy; actually, it requires the same critical skills entailed in identifying weaknesses in your opponent's game. However, as you evaluate more often, you will soon have a great grasp on the adjustments you need to make.

By making the correct adjustments and deciding to hit your second serve first, you're taking a lot of pressure off your second serve. Hitting second serves over and over again is not easy. It takes a toll mentally. The returner feels a lot more comfortable being aggressive with your second serve, especially if he keeps seeing them over and over. You should feel no shame in simply getting a point started. A lot of very good players place their faith in other parts of their game, other than their serve. As you begin to make more first serves, your second serve will get better. It will get better because you are taking the pressure off by making a higher percentage of first serves.

I am not telling you to not go for your first serve (for one thing, your opponent will soon catch on). I am simply saying if you miss three in a row, it's time to hit your second serve first. It won't put you in the grandma's league. It will only win you more matches, and make your grandma very proud.

Al Bello/ALLSPORT

Use your second serve as a first, especially if you are struggling.

Tip #29: Learn when to go for an ace.

Nothing is better than the feeling of hitting an ace. "If only winning points could always be this easy," you think. Unfortunately, most players remember the one ace they hit back in 1976, and, due to that one, have spent the rest of their time on the court making 40 percent of their first serves trying to reenact it. As a teaching pro and college coach, I strongly suggest that the majority of players focus more on their first serve percentage rather than on the amount of aces hit. What good does it do if you hit 10 aces a match, but you struggle to hold serve due to low percentages? However, as a high level player who relied a lot on his serve, I also understand that certain players need to go for aces and have to rely on their serve if they find it to be a weapon in winning free points. Players have to balance when to go for the ace or service winner and when to serve at a high percentage into the body (as I recommend in Tip #15). So when can you go for an ace? I have found three instances in a match where it would benefit you to consider going for an ace.

First, go for an ace when your opponent doesn't expect it. Obviously, your opponent is not expecting you to hit aces very often, but his expectation has more to do with what patterns you have been using up until this point in the match. For example, if the current score is 4-4, 30-all, and you have been serving into the body on every other 30-all point this set, you'd have an opportunity to go for an ace. Your opponent is expecting you to serve where you have served during a similar point/situation in the past. He would be stupid not to. Use the expectation that he has and try to slice an ace out wide, or slam a serve up the "T".

Second, go for an ace when your opponent has gradually changed his return position. It's difficult to track your opponent's position throughout the match because it happens slowly; however, every once in a while, take a step back before serving and ask yourself, "Is he standing the same place he was last game, or at the beginning of the match?" A smart returner will start to move after realizing what your best serves are in order to cover them or take them away from you. As a server, you want the returner to always be guessing and wondering where you will serve. If you notice a drastic change in where your opponent is standing, then fire an ace to the opposing corner to get him back. This play works whether or not you actually make the serve (obviously, making it is preferred). By crushing a serve to the open space of the service box, even if you barely miss, your opponent will be sent the message that he needs to readjust his spacing and you know what's up. A baseball pitcher will throw high heat close to the batters head if he feels he is crowding the plate to get him to move back. Even though it is not a strike, it's an effective play that sets up other pitches. You can do the same.

Third, go for an ace when you "feel it." The first two instances involve your opponent, but the most important time to go for an ace is anytime you really feel like you've got it. I know that advice sounds cliché, but the way you feel before you serve should determine what you do. It's the sixth sense of being an athlete. Learn to listen to yourself, your first instinct, and honor it. Obviously, you will "feel it" more if you are up in score or ahead in the set, but you'll have times when, historically, it's not the right time to go for an ace and you will just really feel like you should. I say, go for it.

Tip #30: Realize that 30-love is overrated.

You're up 30-love. What do you normally try on the next point? Something big, right? Something you ordinarily wouldn't try? If you have that much confidence to go for something big and out of the ordinary, I say do it. However, before you try your drop-shot lob-combo, think about the difference between winning and losing the next point. A score of 30-15 is significantly different from 40-love. At 30-15, you're still anxious to win the game. At 40-love, even the fiercest competitors will slip a little mentally. So, until you develop a huge serve like Pete Sampras or a return like Andre Agassi that can win you free and easy points at 30-15, take extra care of the 30-love point.

I make my life a lot easier by taking a little bit off and hitting a heavy kick or body serve at 30-love. I'm playing the percentages by making sure I make my first serve. If my opponent ends up winning the game, then he has played some great tennis and I could have done very little differently.

Play a high percentage point, make the first serve, and work the middle of the court from the baseline. Nothing fancy. You have your opponent in a tight spot. All you need to do is tighten up your game a little.

If you're up 30-love and returning, do everything in your power to get that first return in play. Then, play strong but safe shots. Make the server feel like he has to do something great to win this game. Be stingy. Give nothing away.

Tip #31: Restart the point by centering the ball.

Whenever two professionals are in a groundstroke battle and one gets pulled wide, he'll throw a high and deep ball towards the center of the opposing court. The ball is high to allow him enough time to recover, getting back to the middle of the court. It's deep so his opponent can't step up and hurt him, and it's in the center so his opponent can't play the angles.

"Here we go again," his opponent thinks, "I have to start all over." He's right. He has basically restarted the point. This play is especially effective for scrappers, pushers, grinders, and counter-punchers. Everybody calls Lleyton Hewitt a "pusher," but he wins, so who gets the final word? Utilize this play to get yourself back in more points, just like he does.

Pete Sampras was magical. However, I don't recommend that the average player emulate his shot selection when he was out of position. He would go for a winner—and amazingly, he would make many of them, developing a running forehand weapon that still gives his competitors nightmares. Just because you hit one astonishing running forehand three years ago doesn't mean you should keep trying to hit it. Instead, work on throwing up a high and neutral ball when you are on the dead run. Have a practice partner feed you a ball and sprint after it. Try to re-center the ball with lots of net clearance and depth.

Too many people actually lower their net clearance when they're on the run. Try this instead: for every foot that you stray away from the center mark, hit the ball one foot higher than your normal shot. Let's say you're eight feet wide of the center line: if your average shot has a net clearance of three feet that means you'll have to hit this shot 11 feet over the net. That height will certainly give you enough time to reposition.

If you can play this ball deep, you can completely neutralize your opponent's attack. By playing the ball in the center, you're only giving him a risky change-of-direction shot if he's determined to play the angles. If the ball is properly played with height, depth, and very little angle, it is very difficult for him to win the point, even when you're on the run.

The point is, keep it simple. Too many players complicate things on the run, going for an unbelievable shot. By re-centering, you're taking your opponent's aggressive shot and saying, "I'm sorry, but let's see if you can do this shot again—unless I get a chance to hurt you first." Soon, your opponent will realize what you're doing. If he's smart, he'll probably sneak into the net to face a high and fairly easy volley. No sweat. Now all you have to do is use the following tip.

Wolverine Photo/Amir Gamzu

Using height on the run is one way to get you back in the point.

Tip #32: Learn the "twice, not once" theory of passing and volleying.

Plenty of players have lots of success coming to the net, even though they don't volley particularly well. These players are called "bluffers." Plenty of pro players "bluff"—they're just better at it. I have been called a "bluffer" by nearly every one of my opponents, but I would still win a lot at the net. Just because a player is at the net, doesn't mean he knows how to (or wants to) volley. Quite the contrary, it simply means they are relying on you to make the mistake when you feel the pressure, and it works. You can hit ground strokes all day, but as soon as your opponent charges, you get tight.

Playing the net is about confidence. It's about having the guts to get in and say, "Let me see if you can handle my net play." Usually, they can't.

If you find yourself consistently having trouble against a net rusher, missing passing shots wide and in the net, the "twice, not once" theory will help. It's simple. Use the first passing shot to set up the second, and winning, passing shot. Think about it. When your opponent comes to the net, when do you usually miss? I'm guessing you miss the first shot, as soon as the pressure is applied. The pressure is the greatest on that first ball. After that point, every volley and passing shot you play feels more comfortable.

By exercising the "twice, not once" theory, you are committing completely to making your opponent hit at least one volley before you go for a passing shot. Instead of panicking and going for a running forehand pass, put the ball back in play, preferably low and in the middle of the court. Recover, and see what your opponent does with the volley. Chances are good the volley won't come back. After all, it takes skill to return a low volley in the middle of the court. If the ball does come back, it is likely you'll then have your best chance at passing.

The fact is, most players do not volley well, and all volleyers hate to hit low volleys. I love coming to net, primarily because I love doing nothing to win a point. My opponents win it for me. It's when I am up against an opponent that makes me play low or even mid-height volleys in the center of the court, point after point, that I know I have to back off a bit. By utilizing the "twice, not once" theory, you force your opponent to beat you. You don't beat yourself. Use your first shot to call the bluff. Then, take the second shot and pass them.

The theory also applies when you come to the net. You want your opponent to play two passing shots to beat you, instead of going for broke on the first volley. Play one volley to set up the second winning volley. When coming to net, plan on hitting two volleys. Unless you are sitting on top of the net for your first put away, put your first volley back deep and into the court, and then get ready to finish with the next. (Tip #18 discusses the proper place to play volleys).

Think of using two volleys to win the point, not one.

Tip #33: Never stand in the same place twice if you're up against a huge server.

Nothing is more frustrating than getting served off the court. You may have a better all-around game, but it doesn't matter if your opponent always holds serve.

When you're playing huge servers, your goal is to get them out of their rhythm. For starters, never stand in the same place twice in a row. Stand in very close, stand back, stand in the alley, stand close to the "T", stand relaxed, or stand intense. Yes, you could end up disrupting your own rhythm and match pace. In this case, though, it's okay. If you are disrupting your own pace, odds are, you are also disrupting the server's.

Put yourself in the shoes of the server. He probably knows where he's going to serve and what to do after the serve is in play (serve out wide and volley, serve into the body and stay back, etc.). When he sees that his opponent is standing someplace abnormal, he immediately has to rethink, and it throws off his rhythm.

The key is inconsistency. Normally we think that consistency, not inconsistency, is essential to successful tennis. However, in the case of returning a huge serve, be as inconsistent as possible with how much time you take in between points and where you stand. Never let the server see that you are annoyed. What does Andre Agassi do after he is aced? He walks to the other side of the court. What about if he is aced again and again? The same thing: no yelling, no tantrum. He just keeps his eyes on the strings and walks to the other side. Don't be freaked out if you still get aced. The effect of disrupting a server's rhythm is cumulative. Sooner or later, it pays off.

Adjust your stance if your opponent is serving bombs.

Wolverine Photo/Amir Gamzu

Tip #34: Intimidate with consistency, not power, if your opponent is a weak server.

Some very savvy and successful players, even pro players, have serves your grandma would laugh at. That fact should tell you that the rest of their game is probably rock solid. It also means you'd better take advantage of their weakness.

The common response to a weak server is to make your opponent eat dust every time he floats that peashooter over the net. I love the aggressive mindset, but hitting winners isn't easy. Before you know it, you've become frustrated and your opponent is probably serving better now that he's ahead in the score.

After recognizing that your opponent has a serving problem, immediately understand that he will also have a phobia about the shot. Store that point in the back of your brain, so that later, you can capitalize on his fears. The best way to hurt and intimidate a weak server is not by trying to blow winner after winner by them, but by simply returning aggressively. Stand inside the baseline, and when that powder puff serve comes floating over the net, play the ball nice and deep, waiting for the right moment to play even more aggressively, and apply the knockout punch. On a big point, step up and attack the serve with a bit more aggressiveness than he's used to. Give a nice loud grunt and look to hurt your opponent. Or, play a normal return up the middle of the court and follow it in to net. This technique can destroy opponents. They already hate to serve and now they're afraid they'll have to pass. Soon, their serving phobia seeps into other parts of their game.

The thing to remember is, playing a weak server is more about executing aggressive plays on big points versus just wailing away on the ball from the first point of the match. Most players on every level give away too many points by trying to crush a bad serve. It is much easier to start a match with consistent returns. Then, once you're in that rhythm, become more aggressive. By saving the aggressive play, you have the element of surprise working to your advantage.

Strong, consistent returns are the best way to hurt a weak server.

Phil Cole/Getty Images

Tip #35: Retrieve a fresh grip and shirt if you've thought about it once.

Tennis is a mental battle. The goal is to keep your mind happy and clear at all times. Do you think that Pete Sampras' mind was racing in a hundred directions before he hit a serve? Not a chance. Sampras knew how to quiet his mind. The best way to quiet my mind is to deal immediately with the little things. For instance, if I think about changing my shirt or grip, I do so at the first opportunity. No debating or indecision. I like my play to be decisive and clear-cut. If it comes into my head once, I deal with it.

You are only as good as your grip. The same goes with shirts. I'm not recommending buying the most expensive shirts, but always carry at least three shirts with you to each match, one for each set. Other players laugh when they see how many grips and shirts I bring to the court, but I want to have enough so that I can make a change the minute my brain thinks "shirt" or "grip."

Everything you do on the court is important. The moment you think about changing your shirt, attach value and meaning to the action. Think, "I am changing my game, I am now coming out fresh, I am now lighter and more agile, I feel more comfortable."

I used to never change my shirt at tournaments because I hated having to wash my clothes. I didn't change my grip because they cost too much. Well, the moment that I started listening to my internal desires and quieting my thoughts, guess what happened? I won more matches. I felt calmer and more confident because I knew that I was doing what I needed. Trust me, doing laundry can be fun if you are still in the tournament.

Sometimes, something as small as changing a grip on a changeover can get you back into the match and playing great again. I am serious. Nothing feels better on the hands than a fresh grip. What kind of mental message are you sending yourself if you change your shirt and your grip before your opponent is trying to serve out the match? What kind of message are you sending your opponent? You are being very direct in telling both yourself and your opponent, "This game is not the last. I am going to break serve and win this match."

Tip #36: Know the six steps to serving out a match.

The most difficult job in sports is finishing off an opponent in a tough contest. Baseball teams pay millions of dollars to "closing" pitchers who might only face one batter a game. Unfortunately, in a tennis match, you can't call the bullpen and bring in your huge server to serve out the match while you stand on the sidelines watching. The best players in the world are the ones that can consistently serve out a match and make the difficult seem easy.

In one of my first pro tournaments, a $10,000 future in Korea, I found myself in the first round of the main draw playing against the previous week's winner. I was up 5-1 in the third and decisive set, holding a double break lead, and feeling good about my chances to serve out the match. To make a long story short, I quickly lost the next game, and the next, and the next, and the next, and the next, and the next. I lost 7-5. Afterwards, I was heartbroken. That night I didn't sleep a wink because I was lying in bed thinking about the match. Finally, I got up, started to write, and drafted this plan.

Step #1: Activate the "now" before your service game by focusing on breathing and heartbeat.

The two most common feelings before serving out the match are complacency and nervousness. It is so easy to think ahead to how happy you'll feel after winning. Guess what? It ain't over. The fat lady hasn't begun to sing. On the other hand, the feeling of nervousness causes tightness and tentativeness. Both complacency and nervousness shift the focus away from the present and into the future, which is into a time that does not exist. Before serving out a match, I focus on two things: my breathing and my heart rate. They bring me to the present moment. Try it now. Listen to your breath and heart by closing your eyes and concentrating on the inside of your body. When you focus on your breathing, you are focused in the present.

Step #2: Walk like a champion: loose, confident, relaxed, focused, and happy.

After intense focus on the now, walk around the court like a champion, take your time, and be sure and cocky. Walk the way you want to play the next game, relaxed yet intense. Roger Federer often bounces the balls between his legs before he serves. This action keeps him relaxed and having fun. "I'm not playing for world peace or a happy life," I think, "I'm just playing a game."

Step #3: Smile and think of something that makes you laugh.

Approach the baseline, ready to serve, with a clear mind. Now, take a second and think of something funny. It feels empowering to be able to smile on the tennis court, especially before you serve the match out. I always think of a time when my sister dumped a full glass of milk on my brother at the dinner table. With that thought, I'm happy, loose, and ready for the next step.

Step #4: Cool yourself down by blowing on your hand and say, "Cool as ice."

Now let's coordinate the mind with the body. I shift the racket into my left hand and lightly blow on the palm of my right hand. "You're as cool as ice," I think. This action reaffirms my confidence and cools me down—or, I feel like it has. Now, I don't go around the tournament telling myself, "You're as cool as ice," but when I am standing on that baseline getting ready to serve out the match, it helps to reaffirm my abilities.

Step #5: Loosen the arm before serving.

Now, take care of the actual serving arm. To combat feelings of tightness, lightly shake your serving arm as if it were a wet noodle, loose and uninhibited. It's a crucial step in coordinating a relaxed mind and body.

Step #6: "Eyes on the prize."

Lastly, as you bounce the ball before your serve, think, "Eyes on the prize." It helps me keep the eyes on what is important, the ball, and not where my serve goes or my next shot. All through the point, think, "Eyes on the prize," and nothing else, because nothing else matters.

I know that they seem drawn out and lengthy, but all six of these steps can be done quickly enough to keep you within the time limit. After developing these techniques, I saw a dramatic improvement in my ability to close out a match. During one stretch, I closed out 37 straight matches. Feelings of nervousness may still linger, but these six steps help turn the negative emotions into positive ones.

Always keep your eyes on the ball—even in pressure-filled moments.

Tip #37: Accept code violations.

Here I am, playing on a stadium court that holds 10,000 people yet only 11 people are watching, and all of whom are cheering for my opponent, a guy known for hooking (cheating). On big points, he calls every ball on the line out. I know that I shouldn't be thinking about the blatant cheating, but it's hard not to, especially when he as much as admits it. After one terrible call, we both met each other at the net, and getting a little frustrated with his calls, I threw a ball at his face. I was then slapped with a point penalty. I was so upset after the whole incident that I lost the next point, the set, and five games that followed. I was down 3-0, two breaks, and all before I really got back into the match. Fortunately, my opponent's only game was a willingness to cheat, and cheating can only get you so far.

My reaction was not one I recommend. Venting and yelling, I let five games slip by. I didn't accept my situation and it should have cost me the match (I was able to win in three).

Tennis can be a frustrating game. That fact is where code violations come in. I have seen nearly every code violation imaginable, and committed many of them myself. I once saw a friend of mine throw his racket over the courts and land in the back seat of a convertible Porsche. Getting a code violation is okay. It is not the end of the world; in fact, it can actually help a player if he's in a rut. Clearly, it is much better to stay calm and compete, but blowing off a little steam doesn't have to be catastrophic. Top pro players get angry, but then what happens? After their code violation or outburst, they usually move on. The difference is how long the negative attitude stays. Andre Agassi might crack a racket over his foot, but he doesn't mope around the court afterward. He doesn't let the outburst control him.

If you are going to be negative, then be "high negative." Let me explain. Once most players get mad, they stay mad for the rest of the match. Nobody is saying that you have to hold in all your emotions, but you should need only one outburst a match. Do it big and then move on. With only one outburst, you are saying, "The way I'm playing is unacceptable. I'm angry, but I will not let that anger influence the outcome of this match. Now I am refreshed and ready to kick your ass."

If you're going to get angry, then accept the consequences and move on. You should know the proper and constructive way to get angry. Yes, a "high negative" reaction will get a code violation because it's going to be noticeable. However, you'll also let go of what was bothering you. The way to win more matches is not to pretend that you won't or can't get mad, because anger is definitely a part of the game. Instead, get mad, and then get over it.

Harry How/Getty Images

If you are going to get angry, that's okay, just accept the consequences.

Tip #38: Focus by controlling your eyes on the court in between points.

If you look up the word "focus" in the dictionary, the definitions involve, "making an image clearer … adjusting for clearer vision." Down the list, you'll find the definition used in sports, which is, "To concentrate or direct attention to." After reading all those definitions, one thing is very clear to me: to focus, you have to control your eyes. Or even better, to focus, adjust what it is that you are looking at. Simple, yet profound. Control what you're looking at to focus on the tennis court.

During a point, obviously you have no choice what to look at. Once the point is over, however, you no longer have a moving ball to grab your attention. You may be distracted by fans, cars driving by, that cute girl who works at the front desk, another match, etc.

So what should you be looking at between points? What do the top men and women do between points? Nearly all of them look at their strings immediately after a point. The ironic part is, they have the most distractions to look at. Thousands of fans, a giant stadium, or celebrities in the crowd; yet, they all look at their strings. Professionals understand the importance of where and how to focus.

The next time you practice, make a point of not taking your eyes off the court until after you're done. You'll see an immediate improvement in your game. Then, for homework, watch a show about wild animals. Where are the animals' eyes as they hunt? Are they looking at the cameraman? No. Their eyes are totally focused on what they are trying to capture, kill, and eat (hopefully it's not the cameraman). Likewise, nothing else but your court should consume you.

Your focus depends on where your eyes are looking. This player is clearly focused on his match, not other distractions.

Tip #39: Stop thinking and start reacting (doubles vs. singles).

I always remember my dad coming home after his singles matches and sitting on the couch, exhausted. He'd sit with a beer in his hand and analyze every point of the match.

"What was the score, Dad?" I'd interrupt, "Did you win or lose?"

"I lost 6-1, 6-1," he'd say.

If this interaction sounds anything like you after a match, I have some advice—stop. Tennis is not war or chess. Tennis is a simple game: who can hit the ball over the net the most times without missing, you or me? Yes, it's important to think during a match, but don't make it any more complicated than it has to be. All you'll do is drive yourself mad.

It is especially true for doubles, which is even simpler. Who makes the most serves and who controls the net—that's it. So, think even less. During the points, your mind should be reacting to the moment. In between, you can quickly assess what just happened. Clearly, if you're getting passed crosscourt every time, do something about it. However, don't start making elaborate calculations while you play. The brain is working even if you are not analyzing the points.

"Well," my dad says, "how am I supposed to know how to win points then?" Easy, use your strengths to win points. Just by being freer on the court you'll win more. No, you won't win every point, but to win the match, you don't need to. It's a simple game and you need a simple game plan.

Notice how the best players in the world look on the court. They look calm and free. Their minds are not thinking about their elbow dropping on the serve or their follow through on the ball. In fact, they aren't thinking about anything. So stop thinking. Start reacting and playing by instinct.

Clive Brunskill/Getty Images

Get your mind out of the way and let your reactions and instincts take over.

Tip #40: Know your game and play it on big points.

When the going gets tough, go with your strengths. You might have spent three weeks working on your weaknesses, but your strengths win matches.

Late in a close major league baseball playoff game, pitchers invariably go with their best stuff—even if the batter is looking for the pitch, the bases are loaded, and the manager is signaling something else. Tennis is the same. On big points, you have to go with your best "pitch." Even if your right-handed opponent has a better backhand return, you have got to go with your favorite serve up the "T" in the deuce court. To do anything else would show that you don't have the confidence in your abilities. If your game is about getting to the net, it doesn't matter if your opponent is a great passer. You need to get in. If your net game is good enough, it should be able to take out any counter-attacker. You have to be confident in your game. When things get uncomfortable, go with what feels comfortable. Don't think about it. Everyone knows that Andy Roddick is trying to hit a big serve and rip a forehand on the biggest point of the match, but what are his opponents going to do to stop it?

Make life easy on yourself when you are faced with a big point. Don't try anything out of the ordinary. Go with what got you to that point. Know your strengths and use them.

3

Match Play: Doubles

Tip #41: Always attack the middle.

Tip #42: Hit your first return up the line and then evaluate.

Tip #43: Use the double play (for the return and net player cross).

Tip #44: Keep moving; never just stand (net and return).

Tip #45: Position yourselves two-up or two-back.

Tip #46: Learn the three most important shots: first serve, first return, and first volley.

Tip #47: Use the "guts" poach (for returner's partner).

Tip #48: Hit at your opponent's right hip on a put away (left hip for a lefty).

Tip #49: Know and utilize formations.

Tip #50: Compliment your partner; never criticize after a bad play.

Tip #51: Laugh on changeovers.

Tip #52: Touch and talk after every point.

Tip #53: Wear something similar.

Tip #54: Take the middle ball when you're the player closest to the net.

Tip #55: Use the "Calkins play" on the second serve.

Tip #56: Learn "Graydon's play."

Tip #57: Isolate the weaker opponent.

Tip #58: Play "one bounce" doubles.

Definitions:

Poaching or crossing: the action of the volleyer (either the server's partner or the returner's partner) when he moves toward the other side of the service line to pick off or volley either a crosscourt return, or a server's first crosscourt hit (a volley or ground stroke). A "poach" or a "cross" is best executed when the returner's/hitter's eyes drop to hit the ball or volley.

Down-the-line return: a doubles return that changes the direction of the incoming serve and is hit at the net player facing the returner. The target of the return is the singles sideline, not the doubles sideline, to give the returner plenty of margin for error. If the opponent moves to cross, the return should be a winner (unless the server is quick enough to get it); however, if the net player does not move, the ball should land safely in and be a volley for the volleyer (not a winner in the alley, which is a very low percentage play).

Tip #41: Always attack the middle.

You've heard it a thousand times. The absolute best place to play nearly every shot in doubles is up the middle of the court, end of story. Volleys, passing shots, serves, overheads, etc., should all be up the middle. Don't just do it once, do it over and over again.

You should play the ball up the middle for a couple of reasons. First, a ball hit up the middle of the court will cross the lowest part of the net, giving you a better chance of making the shot. Second, a ball up the middle creates confusion for your opponents as to who is going to make the play. When you play the ball up the line or to one of the players, it is very clear cut who gets the ball, no confusion. Most doubles players would rather be on the singles court, so test their doubles skills by making them communicate. Third, you'll gain more confidence in your singles play, since playing the middle of the court in a singles match is something that will win more matches.

Stop going for the unbelievable shot in doubles. Doubles comes down to which team can execute the most balls up the middle of the court. Tip #25 ("Angle only if it's a winner") is an absolute must in doubles. Play the middle until you have a clear opportunity to play an angle for a winner. In all likelihood, your opponents will beat themselves before you'll need to hit the winner.

Tip #42: Hit your first return up the line and then evaluate.

I don't like my opponent knowing that I'll hit 95 percent of my returns crosscourt. Therefore, I always hit my first return up the line, straight at the guy standing at the net. I recommend that you do the same. For one thing, you'll find out if he can volley. If he can, then mix things up. If he can't, go at him all day long. Also, by returning up the line, you are forcing him to stay put. He'll hesitate to poach or cross. You have just taken away a favorite play from the beginning of the match, thus creating a bigger target on later crosscourt returns. Finally, it bookmarks the shot for later in the match. A down-the-line return can get you and your partner back in the match. By starting the match with a down-the-line return, you'll feel more comfortable coming back to it. When would you rather hit your first down-the-line return—on the first point of the match, or at 5-5, 30-all?

A down-the-line return early in the match keeps your opponents honest and shows you if he can volley.

Tip #43: Use the double play (for the return and net player cross).

The double play means using the same play twice and on the same opponent. In doubles, it only applies to either the return up the line or the poach (crossing) by the server's partner at the net. Keep in mind that this tip should be used on the same opponent twice, not the next point. For example, you don't use the double play on the second and third point, but on the second and fourth point of a game. Also, it's used on the same person, not the next person.

As I've said, you should return crosscourt nearly all the time. However, if you are getting picked off, it is necessary to return up the line. If the first time you won the point or hit an outright winner, then go back to it again: a double play. Your opponents are probably thinking you won't try to return up the line twice in a row. After all, it's a high-risk play. Even if they were successful and won the point the first time, players like to return up the line about as much as they like to visit the dentist. Use that prejudice to your advantage. Use the double play to confuse your opponent and show the opposing team that you have confidence in all your shots. It's always easier hitting up the line the second time. If nothing else, it keeps your opponent guessing. However, make sure to let your partner know that you'll use the double play so he can expect a volley from the net player instead of the server.

When you're playing the net and are looking to cross, the double play works for the same reasons. If you do cross and are successful once, then cross again when that same opponent returns. The returner will be surprised that you have the audacity to play that aggressively twice. He'll be kicking himself for hitting the ball to you twice. Then, on the third time against that returner, stay home and watch him return to you again, thinking you were going to cross a third time. You have just won three points, off the same returner, and your partner hasn't had to play a first volley once.

Tip #44: Keep moving; never just stand (net and return).

Doubles is all about movement. The team that moves the most wins the most. Doubles players that take over the net also win the most. Players that stay back and play ground strokes watch doubles matches.

Moving doesn't always mean poaching or crossing. At the net, you can jump-stop aggressively right as your opponent's eyes go down for the hit. He'll have no idea what you're going to do, but he can hear your feet and feel your presence. This movement takes his mind off his return. You might cross, or just jump-stop and wait, or just give a very convincing fake. Just standing with no movement, no fake, or no stutter-step won't cut it.

When you're at the net with your partner serving, your goal is simple: do whatever you can to keep your partner from playing first volleys. It's so much easier for you to be an aggressive net player by moving a few steps and crossing to finish off the point than to have your server come running in and play a low volley. It is better to cross and miss than have your partner hit a first volley. By moving, even if you miss, you are sending the message that you are taking over the net. By not moving, the message you send is that you're afraid to volley and won't be poaching for the remainder of the match.

I don't understand doubles players that don't move or cross. Maybe they're afraid of failing or they worry about invading their partner's space. Well, get over it. Your partner hates hitting a volley after serving just as much as you do. If you are aggressive at the net, you'll take some pressure off his volleys and he can concentrate on his serves. Make sure your partner knows that you'll sometimes cross, even if you haven't talked about it. The moving player will take returns at a higher point, which means they are easier to put away.

Obviously, you shouldn't poach on every return. However, if your right-handed partner hits a backhand volley as his first volley in the deuce court, or he hits a forehand volley as his first volley in the ad court (or the opposite if your partner is left-handed), then odds are you should have been able to cross and pick off the return. Both you and your partner should know and practice this technique. Having a specfiic guideline will help facilitate the communication.

Too many players start the match aggressively but taper off as it gets closer and tighter. I suggest the opposite. If the thought of poaching scares you before a big point, do it anyway. It's the right point. Don't just poach on 30-love and 40-15. Poach on deuce, ad-out, 30-all, and 6-6 in the breaker. Take over the match.

You also want to be moving when your partner is returning. If your partner hits a good return and causes the server to hit a low volley, you should cross. It's an excellent opportunity because he'll naturally hit a low volley high. When you do cross, make sure you are moving toward the net, not toward the sideline; that way, you'll be able to cut off more angled volleys. Your target for your volley is the center service line, not the other net player's feet as so many coaches recommend. Better net players who expect the cross will have quick enough reflexes to play your shot back. Make it easy and aim for the middle.

Anytime you see the server play a first volley, you should jump-stop, poach, or fake. Never let the volleyer hit without him seeing you move. Don't feel that it is necessary to always communicate to your partner that you'll be moving. You can still be aggressive without his consent.

The more movement in doubles, the better. Now get going!

Tip #45: Position yourselves two-up or two-back.

What position communicates to your opponents that you're a strong and determined team? You and your partner both up at the net or both back at the baseline, not one up and one back. If both players are not in the same position on the court, the team is vulnerable. Most importantly, the so-called team looks nothing like a team. It looks like two singles players that decided to sign up for the doubles draw at the last minute.

Unfortunately, most tennis players play doubles as if their partner is invading their single's space. However, doubles is a team game. Don't be mad if your partner comes on your side of the court. Playing doubles, you have to move and act as if you are a team, before, during, and after the points. You have to move when your partner moves. If you don't, then you're leaving a vulnerable space open for your opponents to attack.

If one player moves to play a volley in the alley, the other shouldn't stay in his spot, leaving the middle of the court wide open. He should move to the center of the court. If his partner crosses, the server should also cross to the other side; otherwise, he'll be leaving one side of the court uncovered. If one player moves forward from the baseline and takes the net, the other should as well, even if he came in on a terrible ball.

Again, the main objective of any doubles match is to take over the net before the opposing team does. The next best position is for both players to position themselves on the baseline. Having both players back together is better than having one up, one back. For one thing, it's easier to gauge your partner's movement and adjust when you're together. With a team that plays one-up and one-back, a gaping hole is left to be found right in the middle of both players. The middle is the best play to use in doubles and you're asking your opponents to attack it (Tip #41). By playing both at the net, you can plug the middle and force your opponents to hit more high-risk shots. Also, you never want to be looking backwards, watching your partner. Looking backwards is inviting the opposing team's net player to poach and crush you in the face. That mistake won't happen if both players are standing side by side. If you're at the net and your opponent is on the baseline, then you need to yell at your partner to get in as soon as you can, otherwise you're inviting the opposing team to take over the net.

Tip #46: Learn the three most important shots: first serve, first return, and first volley.

Stop having your club pro feed overheads and drop shots. Instead, have him develop your first serve, first return, and first volley. Yes volleys, not ground strokes. One should follow a serve into net because doubles is won at the net, not the baseline.

Playing against some of world's best doubles players is strange. Not a whole lot blows you away. They seldom shock you with unbelievable shots or leave you bewildered with amazing angles and touch volleys. Just the opposite. "Well, they aren't that good," I often think. However, they are that good, and the reason is that they always put the first three shots in play. It's automatic. They might not serve ace after ace or hit volley winner after winner, but they make their first serve, their first volley, and nearly all of their returns, from the beginning of the match through the end.

It's amazing how very few points actually involve more than just the first three shots. You can improve your game enormously by developing those shots alone.

Play "three-shot" sets. If the first serve, return, and volley are not in play, start the point over and do it until you get them all in. You might get stuck on the same point for 10 minutes as a teammate struggles with his return or if the server can't get his first serve in. Eventually though, these three shots will become automatic. They set up the kill shots that win the points. When I first played "three-shot" doubles, I remember thinking, "Why can't we just play normal doubles?" My coach quickly told me I was playing normal doubles because I kept missing. What he was trying to do was get me to play great doubles. Point taken.

You can improve on these three shots even if you can't find three other people to play doubles with. One drill is to play "ghost doubles"—doubles against one other person in which you're playing as if both of you have a partner, but are only playing crosscourt points on half of the court. The center service line is extended to the back baseline, dividing the court into two. The point only continues if the first three shots are executed.

If as a doubles team you can guarantee that you will make the first three shots of the point, you will not only be playing Wimbledon next year, but you will be dancing at the winner's ball. Now get out and do it.

Clive Brunskill/ALLSPORT

If you make your first serve and first volley, you'll be in great shape.

Tip #47: Use the "guts" poach
(for returner's partner).

This tip concerns only the returner's partner at the net. The situation goes like this: it's early in the match and you're at the net with your partner returning serve. The return is in play, crosscourt, but very weak and high, a sure put-away volley by the server. Once the server split-steps and goes to put the easy ball away, you poach. I call this rule the "guts" poach because it takes guts to cross when your opponent is faced with an easy volley that will likely be hit straight at you.

This move might seem impractical, but it pays dividends as the match progresses and things get tighter. You sacrifice the point to show your opponent that you're aggressive and he'll have no easy balls in this match. In this situation, your goal is to simply get a racket on the ball. You shouldn't care if the ball is nowhere close to going in. This is not a play to win a point—this is a play to send a message that you've got guts. Call it an investment plan. You are investing one insignificant point (early in the match) so that every time your opponents hit a volley to that spot, they're just a little worried, and hopefully won't hit the shot as well as they should. What's to lose? If you don't move, you'll lose the point anyway, so poach. Get your racket up and look to stick a reflex volley.

The initial success of the "guts" approach depends on how quick your hands are of course. However, that fact is secondary to the audacious message it sends.

Tip #48: Hit at your opponent's right hip on a put away (left hip for a lefty).

Against a competent doubles team it's difficult to break serve, so when you do get that break point or deuce point, you really have to convert and take advantage. The best way to convert is to have a simple and effective plan of where to hit the ball on those big points.

A short ball is your best chance to win the point. Rip the ball at the weaker volleyer's right hip if he is right-handed, or go at his left hip if he is left-handed. Go at your opponents hard.

Players often blow this easy shot. They try to kill the short ball, hit a cute angle, or go for an extraordinary shot down one of the alleys. Make it easy on yourself, keep the ball in play and aim at your opponent's right hip (if he's right-handed). This shot is not mean. It's smart tennis. The key is to hit the inside area of your opponent's forehand volley. Every tennis player in the world will tell you that the toughest volley to play is one that is aimed for that area. The player's elbow will get in the way of the volley and he has no room to work.

By the way, we're not talking about a basic ground stroke. We're talking about a ball that is sitting up and that you can really crack. It's important that your partner knows where you'll hit these shots. That way, you both will know where to anticipate the weak volley return.

Clive Brunskill/Getty Images

This shot was played perfectly into the right hip, the most difficult volley for a right-handed volleyer to make.

Tip #49: Know and utilize formations.

I recommend three formations for doubles play. Formations are different ways that you can stand to serve and return. You don't have to play the same way every time. You can use different formations to protect your team and utilize your strengths.

Formation #1: Conventional

This formation is the typical position that 99 percent of doubles teams in the world use: the net player standing diagonally in front of the server, facing the returner. This formation benefits teams that serve all over the court and that move across the court to pick balls off. However, if you start to find that you're struggling to make quality first serves, or, more importantly, that your opponents are having a very easy time returning, you'll need to make some adjustments.

Formation #2: I formation

Here, both the server and the net player move closer to the centerline, forming a straight line. Typically the net player has to crouch down lower than the height of the net to keep from getting hit by the serve. The formation works well for servers who primarily serve up the T and to the body. You won't want to hit out-wide serves because the returner can too easily beat the net player up the line. Since it is difficult to take a serve that's up the T down the line, the net player's job is to absolutely smother the net. The I formation works particularly well for athletic, aggressive players who enjoy the challenge of cleaning up the returns. As in any doubles formation, the goal is to keep the server from hitting a first volley. I often times switch from a conventional formation to the I formation when a returner is getting too grooved on our serve.

Formation #3: Australian formation

With this formation, the server and net player are on the same side of the court. The server moves closer to the centerline to shorten the distance he'll have to move to cover the down-the-line return. The net player can either stay in his position, having the server cover the down-the-line return, or poach, leaving the team in a conventional formation. This formation is great for keeping returners from hurting you with crosscourt returns, forcing them to return down the line. Usually, though, they'll hit it crosscourt to the net player, who's ready to volley the ball away for a winner. This formation works particularly well in the ad court against right-handed, one-handed backhands. Many one-handed backhanders have great crosscourt returns, but have difficulty playing the return up the line. By switching to Australian formation, you're not only challenging the returner to return up the line, you're also taking away his best return.

Holding serve in doubles should be fairly easy. By giving the opposition a new look, you will not only throw them off, you'll also incorporate the net player into different formations, forcing him to move and be active.

I recommend two returning formations. The first is the conventional one-up, one-back. You don't want to be in this position very long, however. The returner needs to try to get in, or the net player needs to look to cross and end the point.

If either player or both players are having a difficult time returning, you need to switch to the two-back formation. In this formation, the net player moves back so both he and the returner are standing somewhere near the baseline. The purpose of this formation is to give the returner a lot of leeway in where he can put the ball. Since you're no longer an open target, the opposing team's net player can't volley down your throat. A returner can feel a lot better about where to hit the return because he can hit it anywhere. You can go up the line, lob, or go crosscourt without having to worry whether your partner will get hit. The purpose is to get the return in play, making the opposing team beat you with volleys. The formation is more effective on first serves. On second serves, you'll want to take advantage of a weaker ball. If your opponents hit a low drop volley, it's the responsibility of the player not returning.

Brian Bahr/Getty Images

The I formation is a very effective play.

Tip #50: Compliment your partner; never criticize after a bad play.

Doubles requires constant and honest communication, understanding, openness, and trust. So, you first have to understand the importance of body language. Just saying, "That's okay," isn't enough. You must be sincere. We've all played doubles with someone that says, "No sweat," knowing he doesn't really mean it. Saying that phrase with your shoulders dropped, head down, and mumbling the words communicates a much different message than saying it with eye contact and a positive tone of voice. We communicate over 70 percent of our message through body language, so think about how you'd communicate if you couldn't speak. Stop focusing as much on what you say to your partner and focus more on what you look like when you say it.

Unless you have solid proof that your partner is making mistakes on purpose, don't get angry with him. Doubles is a team game, and losing is never one person's fault. If your partner is playing terrible, you can do things to help. Make more first serves, returns, move more, and help him out.

Compliment your partner not only on great plays but also on errors, especially if it was the right idea. He'll start to feel that it's okay to make a few mistakes. Instead of worrying about messing up, he'll start going for shots.

I am not saying you shouldn't leave room for coaching or helping your partner. After he's missed a shot up the alley, I'll tell my partner that I'd rather him miss up the middle. If he could have poached and gotten the first volley, I'll say so. Just keep in mind, your partner is a human being and isn't tying to lose the match.

Wolverine Photo/Amir Gamzu

Feel free to help your partner out in a positive, complimentary way.

Tip #51: Laugh on changeovers.

The fact that doubles is a team sport and not all about the individual, players should take advantage of having a partner and enjoy themselves. Laugh a little. Have some fun. On the singles court, you can't talk to anybody, which is why when I play doubles, I try to keep it light. I am still very competitive and want to win very badly, but I want to show my partner that I am confident in them, their ability, and that I am having fun, so they should too. Use the changeovers to get to know one another and take your minds off tennis. This tip might sound like advice that contradicts Tip #26 ("Always take the full 90 seconds on a changeover"), but doubles is much different than singles (where strategies and tactics are more complicated).

Doubles is a reaction game. It involves very quick decisions and reflex volleys. Over thinking in doubles is very detrimental. So stop thinking and talking to your partner about every shot. It's okay to talk to him after the points to determine what could have been done differently or why a certain play worked, but on the changeovers, sit back, relax, and laugh a little. Nothing is better than laughing with your doubles partner to help the team bond together and keep the mood light. The following are some topics that I have talked about with my partners on changeovers: what is the best beer in the world, worst loss, best win, longest flight, best football team, funniest travel story, etc. As you can see, none of these have to do with the doubles match that we are playing. Don't worry if you aren't talking about tennis. You only have three questions that you and your partner need to make sure you can answer before you get back out on the doubles court. When you are both on the same page with those three things, than feel free to talk about the stock market or your kids' grades or whatever. The more profound the subject, the better. I once played a tournament in Pittsburgh and played doubles with a German player who wanted to know what the meaning of life was. I'm not sure what the meaning of life is, but to try to find out on a doubles changeover in Pittsburgh is quite profound. So we laughed, and then we won (just like Vic Braden says, "laugh and win").

What are the important questions that you should be able to answer? They are the following: *Who is the weaker volleyer? Who is weaker off the baseline? Who is more prone to move in pressure situations?* If you can both answer those questions and realize what they mean, then take the rest of the changeover and take a break. You deserve it. By knowing the weaker volleyer, you know who to hit to when both players are at net. By knowing the weaker baseliner, you know who to volley to when they are both back. Finally, by knowing who moves the most, you can return and volley to that player's position on the big points.

Stop making doubles complicated. Have some fun on the changeover and laugh. Once it's time to start playing again, quickly snap back into a competitive mode. You'll find that you will feel more refreshed and loose on the doubles court. Take it from me, this is a simple rule that *requires* you to have some fun on the changeover and will improve your game and your team chemistry tenfold.

Tip #52: Touch and talk after every point.

Not talking to your doubles partner during the match would be like a quarterback not calling the play in the huddle. Talking after every point eliminates a lot of the hesitation and speculation as the match progresses. It also helps the team play to each players' strengths. Also, of course, you'll want to get on the same page for the next point. Tell your partner where you'll be serving; that way, he'll know where to expect the return. Likewise, tell him what you plan on doing on a return of serve.

You can spend anywhere from three seconds to all 25 seconds with your partner after a point. You don't have to be best friends. Plenty of good doubles teams play with one another and the players are not friends at all. Just make sure that you're spending some time talking in between points. After the talk, make sure to slap hands, hit fists, or tap rackets after every point.

Watch any other team sport and what do you see? Players are constantly hugging, slapping five, and dancing together. I'm not suggesting you have a choreographed dance after a great play, but don't be afraid to show your partner a little appreciation, especially if he just made a mistake (although a dance would be entertaining).

Slap hands after every point.

Mark Dadswell/Getty Images

Tip #53: Wear something similar.

Since doubles is a team game, you should dress like a team. The way that you and your doubles partner look on the court affects the way that you play.

On the pro tour, doubles players have to look alike. They might not always wear the exact same shirt, but that has more to do with each player's contracts with apparel companies. Even if these rules were not written, I'm sure players would still dress alike because it communicates a very important message: they are a team. Even playing in exhibitions or in money tournaments where these rules don't apply, the players wear similar clothes. You'll be surprised at how dramatically such a little thing can improve you and your doubles play.

Matthew Stockman/Getty Images

Matching shorts and shirt makes a doubles team look like a successful team.

Tip #54: Take the middle ball when you're the player closest to the net.

All too often, a ball will go up the middle for a winner and both players will think, "Wasn't that shot yours?" An easy way to determine whose ball it was is to ask, "Who was closest to the net?" The player closest to the net takes the middle ball for a couple of reasons.

First, the player closest to the net has more of an angle to work with. Think about the angles that you can create at the net versus the angles from the baseline. With more angle to work with, the easier it is to hit a winner and finish the point. However, remember Tip #25 ("Angle only if it's a winner") still applies in doubles play. So don't try a crazy angle if it's not going to end the point. Second, it's an easier volley for the player closest to the net. With one player looking to cover the net (in a two-up position), the other can chase down the lob or hit an overhead, which leads to my next point.

If one player is getting ready to hit an overhead, his partner needs to move toward the middle and be ready to take over the net. Too often a player will hit a good overhead and his partner will just stand back, watching the shot. Odds are the opposing team will get the overhead back in play; so, it's the partner's job to move toward the center, looking to move in and pick off whatever comes back. Playing the net when your partner is hitting an overhead is the most fun job in tennis because you know that you're going to get a high volley to crush. Depending on the strengths and weaknesses of you and your partner, together you can determine where each of you are positioned. If one player has a better volley, then he should be the one to close tighter on the net and his partner should be prepared to run for the lob or hit the overhead.

If you are closest to the net, get the middle ball.

Tip #55: Use the "Calkins play" on the second serve.

Typically, players cross when they're serving. However, you can cross effectively when returning as well. I used this play quite often when I played doubles with my college roommate, Michael Calkins.

If I was playing the ad court at net and Calkins was in the deuce court, he'd run around his backhand on second serve returns and rip a forehand crosscourt. Then we'd both cross. The idea was that his return was strong enough that the opposing team would pop up an easy volley for me to pick off. If the return was not as good as we had hoped or if the opposing player played a tough low volley down-the-line, Calkins was crossing behind me and made the play. I'd cross early to be sure nothing got past me cross-court. Meanwhile, Calkins was covering my original side of the court. The same play will work when returning from the ad court if the returner is very confident in his backhand return (for lefties, it's the opposite on both sides).

Obviously, you and your partner can cross at any time and in any situation throughout your serving and returning games. However, if a returner is running around certain strokes, he won't have to cover as much ground when crossing behind the net player. Nine times out of 10, a second serve to the deuce court will come to a right-hander's backhand or backhand body. By running around the shot and hitting a forehand, you'll be standing near the center baseline. If the server volleys behind your partner, you won't have far to go to cover.

We used this play on nearly every second serve return. Occasionally, our opponents would sneak their second serves out wide, but that's a difficult shot, leading to a lot of double faults. Even if the out-wide serve did go in, I'd stay put and refrain from poaching, so we had them beat either way.

The Calkins play is a great way to break down your opponents' service games. Don't hesitate to run around the shot, crush the return, and cross with your net player. He'll be sitting on top of the net for an easy volley to win the point.

Tip #56: Learn "Graydon's play."

"Graydon's play" is a play that can be used to counter "Calkins play" or completely on it's own. This play is named after Graydon Oliver, another college roommate. Oliver won the NCAA doubles title with Cary Franklin and was ranked consistently in the top 50 in the world in doubles. Let's say it's 30-all (deuce court), you are at net, and your partner puts a somewhat weak second serve into play. With the opposing team's returner running around his backhand (Calkins play), you immediately poach, finding a very manageable volley for the put-away.

Sounds easy right? Well, it is. It's okay to cross on your partner's second serve (even though most club players wouldn't dare do it).

In doubles, anytime a player runs around his backhand (deuce court for righties, ad court for lefties), they're going to return crosscourt. It is just too hard to make that shot up-the-line with your body moving in the wrong direction.

If the thought of crossing scares you, then that means it's a big point, so you need to stop thinking and get crossing. If you are at the net and you see the returner moving around his backhand, than get ready to cross (in the deuce court). When is the best time to go? When the returner's eyes look down to hit the ball.

Wolverine Photo/Amir Gamzu

Once a right-handed player moves around the backhand return, the net player should poach, because odds are the return is going cross court.

Tip #57: Isolate the weaker opponent.

Now, 22 competitors may not be on the playing field in doubles as in football, but twice as many players are on the court as in singles. That number is a big adjustment. You have to use the fact that you are playing a team game to your advantage. Of the two players across the net from you, one is weaker. Hit it to that player. Isolate him. Make him beat you. In doubles, you have no reason to play to the better player.

Now sometimes both players will be at nearly the exact same skill level, but that's rare. Your team's job is to find out who is weaker right away. Who is weaker at the net? Does one have a negligible second serve? Did the guy in the deuce court miss 10 overheads in warm-up? Has he yet to make a forehand? Is he using a wooden racket with no strings? If you aren't able to answer these questions then you need to be paying more attention during warm-up. Now, hit every ball to the weaker player. The only balls that the better player on the court should be hitting are his own serves and returns, the two shots that, by the rules of the game, he is required to play. The weaker player needs to know that you know he's weaker. While you're hammering away at him, the better player is getting frustrated. By the time the weaker player starts to pick it up and the opposing team sends some shots the other guy's way, he's gotten cold.

Keep in mind that it's possible for a very good singles player to be the weaker doubles partner. Singles and doubles are totally different games, so do your scouting with that fact in mind.

Michael Steele/Getty Images

When you have a choice of where to hit the ball, always pick the weaker player.

Tip #58: Play "one bounce" doubles.

People often say, "I know that I should get into the net, but I just don't feel comfortable." Or, "I know we'll win more doubles matches if we get to the net, but I am the worst volleyer."

When I hear that lack of confidence and see that a certain player won't come to net in doubles, I tell them to play "one bounce" doubles. This is a simple and fun drill that will force you to take over the net. If you don't, you lose the point. The game is the same as a normal doubles match except the returning team is only allowed one bounce. They have to let the serve bounce (that's one) and then everyone has to get in and play the point at net.

Players try to lob all the time in this drill because if they land one lob in and it bounces, the point is over. Soon though, everyone's overheads improve so much that the lobbing strategy stops working. You become much more aggressive about poaching and covering the net.

One bounce doubles is also great for improving your singles game. You'll discover quick reflexes you never knew you had. "I never knew that I could volley like that," people say, "I never knew that I was allowed to poach and move all over the court." Unfortunately, in a match, they often revert to the same old tepid baseline game.

If you ever find yourself playing too tentatively in a real doubles match, tell yourself and your partner that you want to play "one bounce" doubles. You'll immediately play more aggressively. After all, doubles is won at the net. If you want to win a doubles match, then you need to be comfortable coming into net and finishing off points.

Daniel Berehulak/Getty Images

As a server, never let the ball bounce to play great doubles.

4

Post-match

Tip #59: Practice after a loss to immediately feel better.

Tip #60: Build on victories.

Tip #61: Stop talking about your losses/loss to other players.

Tip #62: Take three things from each loss.

Tip #63: Accept losing.

Tip #64: Define class and make sure that you lose with it.

Tip #65: Eat something salty within 20 minutes after your match.

What you do after a match is as important as what you do before and during the match. If you've won, then you are still alive, which means you're facing another challenge. "Another day, another opportunity to outperform yourself," a coach used to tell me. The goal is to continue moving through the tournament until you're giving your championship speech. If you've lost your match, you'll want to use the things you learned from the loss to get ready for the next tournament or opportunity in the back draw.

Most of the following tips deal with losing. Most tennis players have no clue what to do after a loss. Most coaches and club pros never help a player learn from a loss. The following is some advice that'll help: a loss is not an attack on your personality and character. It's simply a result that is associated with which tennis player handled the match adversity the best that day. You're not a failure and you're not a loser, you simply didn't win as many sets as your opponent on that day. The better you handle a loss, the better tennis player you'll become.

Tip #59: Practice after a loss to immediately feel better.

"Nothing hurts when you win," Joe Namath said. Well, the opposite is also true: everything hurts when you lose. The great players take a loss hard, but intelligently. They might get ticked off for 30 minutes or so, but then they hit the practice courts. Why? The reason is, losing is a part of tennis.

After I lose a match, I usually feel confused or frustrated with a certain part of my game. How did he make me miss so many balls? Why was I serving so poorly? These are all good questions to ask, and it's right to try to figure out what went wrong. However, feeling sorry for yourself only digs the hole you're in deeper. The best way to stop feeling terrible and start feeling productive about a loss is to get back out on the court and work on something. Get better. Grab a practice partner. Play another set. Have him hit serves to work on your return. Hit crosscourt forehands. Now is the chance to fix whatever wasn't working. You'll walk off the practice court feeling better about your game and yourself. Or, if you can't find a practice partner, find a backboard. If practice courts are not available, you can always find something to do that'll be beneficial.

If someone made me practice after a loss when I was younger, what a difference it would have made in my game. I was often times too stubborn and upset to get back on the court. What's more important than a loss is the way you handle it. The grit it takes to hit the practice courts after a loss will win you more matches in the future.

Cameron Spencer/Getty Images

A loss can sting, but to feel better immediately, get out on the practice courts ASAP.

Tip #60: Build on victories.

Players forget why they won immediately after walking off the court. They're thinking about their next match, or, even worse, they're calling everyone they know. I can't tell you how many times I have seen players on their cell phones before they've even left the court. No cool down, no stretching, and no thinking about the match. You need to use a win to build your confidence by briefly analyzing why you were successful.

Find a quiet place where you can properly stretch and cool down, talking over the match with a coach or somebody who knows the game. Identify things that worked. Think about how you won the majority of the points. Try to come up with three concrete things you can take away from the win and into the next match.

As tournaments progress, you'll find your strengths get even stronger and your weaknesses improve slightly. Focus on your strengths. They're why you're winning. You'll have time to deal with your weaknesses, but not while you're still in the tournament. It's on the practice court, when you're out of the tournament.

Pete Sampras didn't stop serving huge just because he was playing a better returner in the second round than he did in the first round. He made certain adjustments, but stuck with his strengths, using what got him into the second round. Everybody knew how he was going to play. They knew he'd be serving huge and coming to the net, but what were they going to do?

If you won your first match by taking second serve returns early and coming to net, then start your next match by doing the same thing. If you won the pervious match by grinding from the baseline, then that needs to be what you go to at the beginning of the second match. You might have to adjust your game plan if things go sour. However, first go with what got you that point in the first place.

When you win, use that confidence to carry you through the entire tournament.

Tip #61: Stop talking about your losses/loss to other players.

Why do players talk more about their losses than their wins? You should know something about your tennis friends: they want to beat you, otherwise they wouldn't be entered into the tournament. So stop talking to them about your losses. You're only giving them the idea that you're no good.

Don't get me wrong, a time and a place does exist to discuss and learn from a loss. We learn from failure. However, be sure to talk about losses with the right people—your coach, your parents, your siblings, your best friend, or a tennis friend you trust and that knows your game. Your losses should not be the general topic of discussion at the clubhouse card table.

Don't feed the competition with ways to beat you and don't show them that you're not confident in your game. A tournament can be a difficult environment with every player asking about your results and your ranking. It's all garbage. Talk about a loss to improve your game. A champion doesn't deny that a loss occurred, but if he's trapped to talk about a sore subject, then he does so with class and confidence. Champions talk about what they learned from the loss, not how they failed to close it out.

We all know players who pretend to be your friends but want nothing more than to watch you fail. Unfortunately, tennis lends itself to that sort of insincerity and selfishness. Choose the friends you talk to openly about your weaknesses and losses with care.

Also, talking about your losses to other players opens wounds and keeps them from healing. It's inevitable that others will bring up tough matches. React the way a champion would react. If you've given the game your all, you have nothing to be ashamed of. It's natural to feel angry and upset after a loss. Go off in a corner by yourself. Take a walk or quietly stretch down. Then, get over it. Let it go. Losses happen. Be mature. Show your competition that you're staying positive and working hard.

Tip #62: Take three things from each loss.

Nothing reflects a person's true character better than the way he handles a loss. Naturally, the last thing you want to do after losing a match is to write down three reasons why you lost. However, try not to take the loss personally. Instead, look at it analytically. A loss can be more beneficial than a win, especially for juniors developing their game.

You want to rationally evaluate both your play and your opponent's play. These observations should be written down. Don't think that you can just remember what to work on. If you keep a journal, eventually, you'll have page after page of areas where you need to improve.

By taking a look at your opponent's tendencies, you're essentially looking at how he exploited your weaknesses. Was he finishing points at net, on the baseline, or by serving aces? If your opponent was covering the net like a madman, maybe you weren't hitting the ball deep enough. Maybe your second serve was sitting up, allowing him to hurt you. Probably the most important question that you can ask yourself about your opponent's play is, "How was my opponent holding serve?" Odds are, if he won, he was holding frequently. Was he on fire or were you simply missing lots of returns? Why weren't you forcing any break points or at least forcing your opponent to play some pressure points while serving?

Now look at your own play. How were you winning points? Was your opponent hitting unforced errors or were you forcing them? How were you holding serve? What happened on the games when you got broken? You have two different ways to lose a point in a tennis match. Either your opponent has won a point or you have lost it. In other words, the error is either forced or unforced.

Only people destined for failure will let the same mistakes beat them again and again. The more serious you are about your game, the faster you'll learn from your losses.

Tip #63: Accept losing.

I have written a lot about losing. Why do you think that is? Have you ever known a tennis player that hasn't lost? No matter how good you are, even if you are ranked number one in the world, somebody can always be better than you on a given day. Top-ranked players lose all the time. It takes a mature competitor to really learn from a loss. Nobody likes to lose, but if you're truly committed to being a great tennis player, you have to do the right thing for your game and your body all the time.

In the poem "If," Rudyard Kipling writes, "If you can meet with triumph and disaster. And treat those two impostors just the same…." These lines are written on the wall of the entrance to center court at Wimbledon. Is it possible that the key to tennis success is written above the entrance to the most coveted and honored tennis court in the world? Yes it is. The players privileged to walk out onto center court at Wimbledon have learned how to handle winning and losing. They treat both those impostors the same. They practice the same and compete the same if they're winning or losing.

If you lose, don't question your ability or feel sorry for yourself or think that your game is terrible. Accept the loss and move on. You might be thinking of the famous quote, "Show me a man who doesn't care if he loses and I'll show you a loser." I agree. You *should* care if you lose. It should hurt, but it shouldn't break your spirit.

The best players have very short memories when it comes to their losses. You should too. If you accept the fact that you'll lose, what is there to fear? The worst thing that can happen to you is a loss. So what? Wouldn't it feel great to walk on the court and not fear anything? The irony is that the moment you accept losing as a part of the game, your game will pick up. Soon, you won't lose as often. Go figure.

Phil Cole/Getty Images

Accept losses and move on.

Tip #64: Define class and make sure that you lose with it.

If you lose with class, you'll always be a winner. Most coaches can only teach their students how to play tennis (and some can't even do that), but if they spent more time teaching class, they'd see an important change not just in their player's attitude, but also in the level of their games.

One of the things that college tennis taught me was that the better the player, the less he cheats. My freshman year I played #6 singles (the lowest position on the team), which you soon learn is less about tennis talent and more about handling cheaters. I hate to admit it, but I have won matches in which I made terrible calls. Even though I won, I now think that I really lost. After all, what is more important, the score of the match, or the way you feel about yourself? In 10 years, will either my opponent or I remember the score? Or, will we both remember that I cheated him with a terrible call?

The better the player, the more class he has. He understands the essence of the game: a competition that depends on cooperation and respect. Once I realized this fact, my game improved. To be a better player, I had to sacrifice some competitive anger and compete with more class. Think about it: would you be making those same calls if your son or daughter were watching? Despite the "winning isn't everything, it's the only thing" attitude, the truth is, to lose with class matters infinitely more than winning without class. If you lose with class, it will sting for a while. If you don't lose with class, it will not only sting forever, but that same classless behavior will seep into your entire personality.

What would you rather be known as, the top player at your club who cheats or as an honorable competitor? Making the right line-calls is a start, but it doesn't mean you're competing with class. Think about what you want people to say about you and your game if you're not standing next to them. You need to live up to that image every time you step on the court, which is especially true when you lose. Winning with class is easy. Ultimately, when you compete with class, you are taking enormous amounts of pressure off yourself. You're acknowledging that tennis is a privilege to be respected and enjoyed, and that win or lose, you should have no shame in your game.

Tip #65: Eat something salty within 20 minutes after your match.

This tip won't help you play better tennis today. It will, however, help you play better tennis tomorrow.

Eating a small salty snack within 20 minutes after a match (say, a few pretzels) decreases your chance of cramping and refuels your body for the next day. The key is to consume something while your body is still warm and your metabolism is still high (while you are stretching or cooling down). Anything you put into your stomach will metabolize immediately and will cause you to need less fuel to recharge the next day. So, you won't need the normal six bowls of cereal the next morning. A lack of sodium causes muscle cramps and the salty snack helps replenish the sodium you lost in your match.

5

Practices

Tip #66: Watch how rarely the pros miss in the net.

Tip #67: Change your tension when all else fails.

Tip #68: Practice your overhead.

Tip #69: "Catch" the ball to improve volleys.

Tip #70: Use singles sticks (when playing/practicing singles).

Tip #71: Play on different surfaces.

Tip #72: Cross-train on soft surfaces.

Tip #73: Practice in percentages.

Tip #74: Develop a second serve that holds up.

Tip #75: Observe your non-dominant hand.

Tip #76: Watch the ball hit the strings.

Tip #77: Grunt.

Most tennis books focus on training. This book is not one of those. This section looks at things that I have done to get more out of my practice sessions.

I have never met a successful tennis player that doesn't practice. I've heard stories of top players hitting for only 30 minutes a day or taking weeks away from the game, but when they were climbing the rankings, you can bet they were practicing hard.

The practice court is where a great tennis player is made. You don't have to double your on-court time or pay more money for lessons. Just incorporate any one of these tips into your practices. Quantity does not beat quality when it comes to tennis training.

Tip #66: Watch how rarely the pros miss in the net.

The average tennis player takes the wrong things from watching tennis on TV. Inspired by the pros, the average player tries to hit 130 mph first serve aces, rip returns for winners, or hit ridiculous jump overheads. Let the pros hit those shots. What the viewer needs to worry about is trying to get his game as solid as the pros, not as fancy or aggressive.

The next time you watch tennis on TV, notice how rarely the pros miss in the net. Some of the best players will go sets without missing in the net. Now, the next time you are at your club, ask yourself who will miss in the net first. You won't have to wait long. It'll probably happen right away. The pros still lose points of course, but rarely by hitting in the net. Amateurs, on the other hand, lose nearly every point by hitting straight into the net.

Have you ever played tennis without a net? Probably not. So learn from the best players in the world and stop hitting into it. Get maximum net clearance. The pros will hit any ball up the middle of the court at least two or three feet over the net.

Whether you're eight or 80 years old, man or woman, the better you are, the less you miss in the net. While you drill, raise the net or string something across the court two feet above the net. Keep in mind, you still want to rip it, but rip it high and clear of the net.

When I give lessons, the player and I will warm-up for the first 10 minutes, hitting back and forth. After 10 minutes, I call the player up to net and tell them to look around. Usually about 15 balls are on his side of the net and none on mine. Once he sees for himself the error of his ways, guess what happens? His net misses decrease immediately and dramatically. I didn't change his strokes, his string tension, his footwork, his outfit, or his fitness. All I did was challenge him to focus on net clearance. If you miss in the net often, it is possible that you have a swing or footwork problem, but odds are you are just not concentrating hard enough. Get the ball up.

Instead of noticing all the spectacular shots the top players hit on TV, I'd love to hear one player come up to me and say, "Serena Williams only missed three balls in the net last night." Now that player is learning from the pros.

Tip #67: Change your tension when all else fails.

Instead of switching rackets every six months to the newest and latest stick, try switching your string tension. A new racket does not change your game. A new racket only changes your perception of your game, and eventually you are right back where you started.

Big topspin string, gut, synthetic gut, polyester, touch, soft, hard, 16 gauge, 17 gauge, etc.—you name it, they've got it. Strings are important, but worry more about your tension. The tension can seriously change the way the racket plays. It's why players always seem to love the newest club demo racket: its tension is different. The rule of thumb for string tension is, "Higher (i.e., tighter) for more control, lower for more power." A racket strung at 80 pounds will have a very high "ping" and you'll really have to swing hard to get the ball to go anywhere. A racket strung at 40 pounds will feel like a trampoline, generating a lot of power. No "right" string tension exists. Some pros string tightly (75 pounds) some string looser (50 pounds). It just depends on what feels right for each player's game. Changing your string tension can make a huge difference in the way that you play.

Getting a racket restrung can be expensive ($30), but you should do it at least twice a year if you play two to three times a week. Playing tennis with a freshly strung racket is a great feeling. The ball feels much crisper, it comes off cleaner, and the racket feels newer. A new tension can give you a new way to play and can help certain areas of your game. If you're emphasizing more serves and volleys, you'll want to string looser. However, on a slow court or clay court, you'll probably want to raise the tension so you can rip balls from the back without worrying about flying the ball over the fence.

The point is, switch things around. Certain tensions will complement your strengths and accentuate your weaknesses. Others will help cover up your weaknesses, but won't do anything for your strengths. Find the one tension that's best suited to you and the environment you're in.

Tip #68: Practice your overhead.

The overhead is one of the least practiced shots in tennis and probably one of the easiest to do. People who suffer from a poor overhead, despite having good volleys, will avoid the net because all the opponent has to do is throw up an easy lob. Improving one's overhead can dramatically improve your confidence in your net play.

I have found the best way to improve your overhead is to simply practice more of them. I see players spend 30 minutes working on their forehand and 30 seconds hitting overheads. The following is a simple, competitive drill that will force you to hit more overheads. It is called (thanks to my creativity) the Overhead Game.

Have your practice partner stand in one corner with you in volley position. The baseliner (your opponent) can only hit lobs, you can only hit overheads. Your opponent feeds in a difficult lob (vary the level of difficulty depending on the level of player you are) and you hit overheads to that corner for the remainder of the point. The goal for the baseliner is to work on his/her defensive lob, moving the ball around the court. The goal for the hitter is to make as many aggressive overheads and when finally earning a shorter, easier lob, have the ability to put the ball away. Play games to seven, then have the baseliner come to net (switch roles). Compete to both the ad and the deuce court. Four games to seven will take about 15 minutes and will result in approximately 75 overheads a player. All those overheads make for a great practice.

Two high-level players will play one point with 10 to 15 overheads. Are you able to be that consistent with your overhead? It is difficult to win the game by only hitting to one corner of the court, but rest assured, you will feel much more confident when you are in a match and you can hit the overhead to either side of the court. The players I coach play the Overhead Game two to three times a week, and I have seen dramatic improvements in their ability to finish points at net. You will come to the same conclusion.

Tip #69: "Catch" the ball to improve volleys.

Putting your racket aside, stand on the baseline empty-handed. Now, have somebody feed you a first volley as you're coming to the net. Catch the ball with both hands before the ball bounces and continue to move forward as you would in a match (if you are hitting against the wall, simply hit a shot, drop your racket, and move forward to catch the reflected ball).

This easy drill is great for three reasons: one, it forces your feet to keep moving forward before, during, and after the volley; two, it keeps your hands together, where they should be; and three it forces you to focus your eyes where your hands are.

Reason #1: You want to keep your momentum moving through the volley.

If you're running forward and trying to catch the feed from your practice partner, your feet will naturally carry you forward. Think of an outfielder catching a short fly ball. He moves forward after the catch. The first volley on the tennis court is exactly the same. Yet, a lot of players run up to the net and play their first volley by stopping all their forward momentum. Usually this move means they have to move forward again—to pick up their volley out of the net. The forward momentum translates into a deep and penetrating volley. You're also closing in on the net, making your opponent feel your presence, which is how net points are won.

Reason #2: You want your hands together for a volley.

Your hands move together. Take a low volley and put both the racket-face and your hands close to the ball, just as you do on high and midlevel volleys. The way your hands operate when you catch a ball is similar to how they work when you volley. Eventually, as you get better, your non-dominant hand will move away from the contact point for balance, but for now, try to keep the hands together.

Reason #3: Your eyes should be where your hands are.

The head should be close to the contact point. This action not only allows you to watch the ball properly but also coordinates the entire body. When you go to catch the ball in this drill, you'll naturally bring your eyes close to the catching point because your hands and the ball are small and you need to watch closely to make the catch.

With your practice partner feeding you high, mid-level, and low volleys, catch 25 balls before you pick up a racket. Then, as you start to actually hit volleys, pretend the racket is no longer in your hands and you still have to catch the ball. You'll see a dramatic improvement.

Tip #70: Use singles sticks (when playing/practicing singles).

In order to feel the most comfortable while competing, the court you practice on should be the same as the court you compete on. The closer you can mirror your competitive court while practicing, the better. You wouldn't want to practice on a court that has a service line six inches shorter than a normal court right? So why practice with a net that is lower than the one you will be competing with? Unfortunately, tennis players around the world make this mistake every time they step on the court to practice singles, which is why I recommend using singles sticks when you practice. The singles sticks raise the height of the net, making your practice court more realistic to the competitive court that your tournaments are held on.

At Michigan, we always include singles sticks with our practices. We have found it has dramatically improved our players' understanding of the court. While using singles sticks, it becomes even more obvious that the best choice for many shots is simply over the lower part of the net (crosscourt). This point is an important lesson for any tennis player to learn.

While serving, singles sticks can really improve the understanding of how difficult it is to hit the out-wide serve. Serves that would normally go in, or barely skim the net, are now missing into the net quite decisively. These misses cause our players (and will help you) to realize how important it is to choose your serving targets wisely, and if you do hit the serve out wide, to make sure you clear the net by a significant amount.

Singles sticks make a very small difference in the net height (six inches to be exact), but an important one nonetheless. Take pride in taking care of the small details of your practices and you will find confidence when they pay off in the competitive environment. Singles sticks are exactly 36 inches in height (the same as the net post) and can be purchased at any retail tennis store or made simply from a piece of wood.

Tip #71: Play on different surfaces.

Why is America playing competitive tennis almost exclusively on hard courts? Take a look at the junior national tournament schedule or the USTA league match schedule or the collegiate schedule. Every match is on hard courts. In contrast, Europeans train on a hard court one day, on indoor red clay the next, and on a synthetic grass court the third.

Different surfaces mean softer surfaces, and those are easier on your body. Try playing a three-set match on a hard court and then play a three-set match on a soft clay court. You'll notice a huge difference the next day. The body can only take so much pounding. A softer surface will also improve parts of your game. A clay court improves your ground strokes. Grass or quick indoor surfaces develop volleys and returns. A hard court develops a more well-rounded, all-court game.

So rather than spend $80 on the next lesson, pay $40 to play on a different surface. Be creative in finding alternative places to play. Once a month, play at a different club. Its courts might still be a hard surface, but they play at a different speed. Even some courts at the same club will be faster or slower. Any variation will go a long way toward improving your movement, fitness, and shot-making ability.

Daniel Berehulak/Getty Images

Prioritize playing on softer surfaces like grass or clay. Both will develop different parts of your game, while also keeping the pounding on your feet to a minimum.

Tip #72: Cross-train on soft surfaces.

Since you probably have little choice but to play a majority of your matches on hard courts, be sure to do your cross-training on a soft surface. You don't have to hit every day to be a great tennis player. Certainly, at some point, when tennis gets more serious to you, you'll want to develop a detailed practice plan and hit every day. In the meantime, you should be getting in shape, but in ways that don't add undue stress to your already battered legs. Either keep your weight off your legs altogether by swimming, lifting, spinning, or riding a bike; or, play sports like Frisbee, sand volleyball, rollerblading, ice-skating, or golf that involve much less pounding of the joints.

How can golf help your tennis? It challenges your ability to concentrate, to execute, to relax, and to perform under pressure. How about Ultimate Frisbee? It offers a very tough workout, but because it's fun, you'll probably push yourself harder than you would in the gym by yourself.

If you're only exercising on hard surfaces in addition to tennis (say, running on streets or playing basketball), it's only a matter of time before you'll seriously injure your body. Too many coaches and players are convinced that your physical fitness routine has to be brutal to be effective. This strategy is far from the truth. Choose a fitness routine that you both enjoy doing and that works your body hard. This routine can be yoga on Monday, pick-up soccer on Wednesday, and spinning on Friday. Your workout won't be something you dread, but instead, something you actually look forward to. This enjoyment will only help your tennis game.

Spinning is a great workout and keeps the pounding off your feet and body.

Tip #73: Practice in percentages.

I recently heard a story about Pete Fisher, the childhood coach of Pete Sampras. He supposedly had divided the game of tennis into percentages and then would spend that percentage of time of practice on Sampras' game. His percentages were as follows: 33 percent of the game of tennis was the serve, 33 percent of the game of tennis was the return, and the last 33 percent was everything else. Think about it. It makes perfect sense. Most of tennis is just serving and returning. Do you have any doubt why Pete Sampras became one of the best players ever?

Yet why do you spend 80 percent of your private lesson hitting forehands and the last 10 minutes hitting a few serves? Start your lesson with your serve, then go on to the return, and if you have time left, work on everything else. The serve and return are the most important shots in tennis. So work on those shots. Stop working on the forehand lob, the backhand volley, or the between-the-leg passing shot. If you develop a great serve, you won't even need those shots, and practicing serves is easy. You can go out to any court at any time with a bunch of old balls. Work on moving the serves around the boxes (deuce and ad court), from the wide serve to up the "T". Experiment with spins and mix in first and second serves.

I have a drill in which I serve out an entire set, me versus my percentages. I start on the deuce side and if I make my first serve where I had previously decided to hit it, I win the point. If I miss my first serve, I lose the point. I then hit a second serve, and if I make that one, I move on to the other side down 0-15. If I happen to double fault, I lose two points, so then the score is 0-30. Pretty easy, huh? Plus, you can usually do this drill for free. Most clubs will let you hit serves on an empty court for free (who cares if the lights are out?).

Practicing returns is a little different. You'll need somebody to hit you serves, which can be easier than you supposed. If he doesn't have a great serve, have him stand at the service line and serve to both sides. Mix up your returns. Go for drives and loops. Have the server hit to your forehand and backhand. I do sets of 10 on each side and keep track of my score. Anything under seven means I have to redo that side. Pete Sampras didn't have the world's greatest return, but he certainly put the returns in the court when he needed to. Was that luck or a testament to his coach hitting him serve after serve when he was a kid?

Spending too much time on the wrong parts of the game is something that every coach, including me, is guilty of. A lot of pro players have nothing but either a great serve or a great return. Yes, some players (and all in the world's top 20) have amazing all-around games, but you can get very far in tennis if you have just a great serve or great return. So start spending the appropriate amount of time on these shots. You'll see a dramatic improvement overnight, and so will your competition.

Tip #74: Develop a second serve that holds up.

You've probably heard it a thousand times: "You are only as good as your second serve." We all know the player that has a good all-around game and even a good first serve, but his second serve is powder puff. Against any competent player, he'll lose because eventually, at a crucial part of the match, he'll be forced to hit a second serve under pressure. The key is developing a second serve that will not only hold up under pressure but will also help you win points.

The following drill can be done on any court at any time. Before beginning the drill, the player must think of a consequence for a missed serve. After deciding on your consequence, take 10 balls and line them up on the ground behind you. Now try to make 10 out of 10 second serves, alternating from the deuce court to the ad court. Any serve that is missed is noted, but continue to hit all 10 serves to end up with a final score. In my case, I would run two laps on a track (a half-mile) for every missed serve. So if I made eight out of 10 second serves, I'd have to run a mile. I might do this drill five times, and every time I'd have a new exercise assigned (20 push-ups, 40 crunches, five pull-ups, five sprints, etc.). After the five drills, I'd go to the track or workout area and do my "punishments." Some days I'd only need to do one set of something, having made 49 out of 50 second serves. Other days, I'd spend an hour on the track because I only scored 35 out of 50.

The point is, you need a consequence for missing because you need pressure to make the drill effective. In a match, you receive a penalty for missing your second serve—you lose the point (if not the game, the set, or the match).

The key to this drill is walking from the baseline back to the line of balls and grabbing only one ball. This action builds suspense and pressure as you see the line dwindling down. You think you won't feel pressure just because it's practice? Making the first and second serves of the drill are always the easiest. Making the ninth and tenth are always the hardest. It's the difference between hitting second serves at one-all in the first versus five-all in the third. By alternating sides of the court, you are rehearsing what you do in a match. You are making it tough on yourself.

Try to stay away from merely pushing the ball over the net. If you need to lower your "punishment," then do so. The first priority is obviously to get the second serve into the court, but as you play better players, you'll need to also hit a deep second serve. Deep second serves can be accomplished by putting down depth targets. Also, don't forget to mix things up. Learn to place your second serve.

Clive Brunskill/Getty Images

You are only as good as your second serve, so work on it.

Tip #75: Observe your non-dominant hand.

Some players have two forehands, hitting with both the right and left hand, but they are extremely rare. The rest of us have one dominant hand. However, just because you're right-handed doesn't mean your left hand isn't important. If you want to improve every single shot in your game, from the serve and forehand to the overhead and volley, focus on what your non-dominant hand is doing during the hit.

The average human arm weighs 15 to 20 pounds. Combined, your arms weigh between 30 and 40 pounds. Next time you are working out, grab a 40-pound dumbbell. It's a lot of weight—and a lot of possible force. So can you imagine how a 15-pound arm moving in the wrong direction could hamper your ability to get the most out of your shots?

It's a very simple rule. The opposite hand travels with the hitting hand. So, on a right-handed forehand, the left hand is traveling close to the right hand, from the preparation to the contact point. What makes a two-handed backhand work so well is both hands work together. The shoulders turn as they should, the hips coil, and you hit with the force of both arms. When you hit a forehand ground stroke or forehand volley and your non-dominant hand is just hanging down at the side of your body, you're not getting a shoulder turn or coiling the hips and torso. To make matters worse, you have a 15-pound dumbbell pulling your body in the wrong direction.

The non-dominant hand determines the success of the serve as well. Anytime you miss a serve into the net, I'd be willing to bet it was because your non-dominant hand came down too early, in which case you're dropping that whole side of your body. The same goes for the overhead. The longer your left hand stays up, the better.

If you have a one-handed backhand volley, the opposite hitting-hand plays a huge role. As you make contact with the ball, both hands should be side by side, almost touching each other. Some coaches advise separating the hands after the hit, which can help; however, before and during the hit, both hands and arms should be next to each other.

If it helps, think of how a grand slam champion holds up the championship trophy with both hands. Only a young Boris Becker tried to hold the Wimbledon trophy one-handed—and he dropped it.

Notice how the left arm is in the proper position.

Donald Miralle/Getty Images

Tip #76: Watch the ball hit the strings.

I know what you are thinking. Ever since you picked up a racket, you've been told to watch the ball hit the strings. Well, guess what? You're still not doing it. Instead of watching the ball, you're watching where you want the ball to land.

Okay, you have a short ball with your opponent completely off the court. All you have to do is tap the ball into the open court for the winner, but your opponent pretends to move, and well, that's all it takes. You miss the easy put away. Sound familiar?

Something as simple as watching the ball hit the strings will improve your tennis immeasurably. It starts in practice and carries over into matches. Before a big point, have your only goal be to keep your eyes on the ball and on the contact point, even after the hit. Your natural competitive drive will still do everything it needs to help you win the point. By giving yourself a simple reminder to watch the ball, you're taking a pressure-filled point and simplifying it.

Watch the pros, especially in a slow-motion replay: they take care of the shot, not worrying about their opponent. They have their eyes fixed on the contact point well after the hit. Roger Federer does this maneuver better than anybody. Any coincidence as to why he is the best player on Earth?

When you get up to the line to serve, you should have an idea of where you are trying to hit the serve. Your brain and your body both know the target that you've selected. However, if you look too quickly to see where your serve went, you'll pull your body down and you'll drive the ball into the net. This mistake is especially common on big points. So again, focus on one simple thing: eyes on the ball! Your body knows when it's time to see where the ball has landed.

I do a drill where I hit serves on a backboard, yet I keep my eyes looking at the contact point until I hear the ball hit the wall. I then get ready to play the ball, and I have plenty of time to do so.

By keeping your eyes on the ball/contact point during and after the contact, you're forcing your head to stay still through the hit. You're also not thinking about the score or where your ball lands. Instead, you're only focusing on executing a proper tennis shot.

Top players say that when the match gets tight or when they're faced with a huge point, they'll remind themselves to only focus on two things: First, have very bouncy, energetic feet. Second, watch the ball closely as it hits the racket. Elementary tennis.

Nick Laham/Getty Images

Your eyes should be on the ball and contact point before, during, and after contact.

Tip #77: Grunt.

You can close your eyes and identify the nationality of a player just by listening to his grunt. South Americans have longer-winded grunts. Americans give a strong emphatic "Eh!" The English never grunt. I contend that it helps your game to grunt. The higher level of the tournament, the louder the practice courts will be.

The grunt serves the same function as exhaling when you're lifting weight. You can hit the tennis ball harder if you're grunting, or at least exhaling, as you hit the ball. As you exhale, the body relaxes and loosens up, allowing for a more free and smooth swing. Also, if you're grunting, you know you're fighting, scrapping, attacking, and doing everything you can to try to win the match. If I'm having a hard time getting my feet and game going, I'll simplify everything and just tell myself to grunt. It also works in practice. When you exhale at the moment of contact, you are simplifying the game of tennis into just one thing: the racket on the ball. You won't be focused on being up or down a match point, getting tight, or on the ankle you sprained last week.

Grunting shows your opponent and those watching that you're a ruthless competitor. I have lost matches before I even stepped on the court because a player has intimidated me. I've heard his grunt and imagined that he crushed the ball. Use the grunt to your advantage, but forget the competition: the grunt sends a great message to yourself, combating self-doubt, anxiety, and nervousness. Don't just take it from me. Ask all the top pros you hear grunting on TV.

Daniel Berehulak/Getty Images

Grunting communicates intensity to not only your opponent but also to yourself.

6

Tournament Environment

Tip #78: Play in environments that complement your strengths.

Tip #79: Know the ball.

Tip #80: Know the supervisor's name and make sure that he knows yours.

Tip #81: Speak confidently about your game and your chances to others.

Tip #82: Accept the draw.

Tip #83: Let others complain.

Tip #84: Listen more and talk less to other players.

Tip #85: Recognize how other players view you.

Tip #86: Spend money on anything tennis related.

Tip #87: Stop giving away your secrets.

The tournament environment can be anything from the players' lounge and hotel lobby to the airport or opening ceremony dinner. I once sat on a flight with 17 other players that I'd be competing against in the upcoming week. To me, that airplane was the same as the tournament players' lounge. I define the tournament environment as any place where you'll find other competitors.

Around your competition, you want to behave the way a champion behaves. Obviously, it's important to get along with others. However, it's not your number one priority to be the most popular person at a tournament. Too many players associate the tournament experience as a social get-together. Leave the social stuff for when you're away from the courts or when the tournament is over. The fun times need to be had away from the tennis courts, at least while competitive matches are in play.

Most players give too much away. They talk to other players about all their recent losses, reasons why they lost, their injuries, why they hate the conditions, etc. Just be friendly, smile, say hello, and then hit the practice courts. Keep your opponents guessing by not telling them anything.

Tip #78: Play in environments that complement your strengths.

The best part about being a professional tennis player is that at the beginning of the year, you get a giant schedule for the upcoming year with hundreds of tournaments around the world, and you get to pick where you'll go. Along with total prize money for the tournament, the schedule lists the court surface, the importance of which most rookie players underestimate. They think, "Oh, I have never been to Japan, that will be exciting." Instead, they should be thinking, "Omni courts? What are Omni courts? I need to learn more before I book my ticket." (Omni courts are synthetic grass covered with sand and only exist in Japan.) A professional tennis player should pick tournaments, environments, and court surfaces that suit his game. You need to do the same.

Choose tournaments where you'll play your best, in an environment that complements your strengths, not one that neutralizes or takes away from them. Let's say you have a successful counter-attacking game. You love hitting on the run because of your great speed. Knowing this fact, you'll want to play tournaments on a medium to slow hard court. The hard court will allow your opponents to try to dictate during the points. A slower hard court will slow down their penetrating shots while giving your feet plenty of traction. Ideally, you'd prefer a heavy ball and to play in "thick air," or as close to sea level as possible, where huge serves move through the air more slowly. On the other hand, if you're a huge server with a great first volley but aren't as confident in your ground strokes and returns, a grass court or fast indoor court will work best for you. High altitudes are also great for huge servers because the ball travels though the air so much quicker, which will further strengthen a strong serve.

If you are playing a tournament and are in charge of booking the court, as is common in many local recreational tournaments, then find the speed of the court that best suits your game and hold your match on that court. It's not cheating. It's being smart and utilizing your strengths. Just because you don't play on a lot of different surfaces doesn't mean that you can't sometimes choose a place to play that's to your advantage—your home club, for instance. People always play better in environments where they feel most comfortable.

Playing futures and satellites, I learned how tough it is to play well the first time in a new environment. It helps to know what to expect. You might have the decisive league match at your opponent's club next week. Having never played at that location, you should book a practice court before the big match. It will make a huge difference.

Pete Sampras lost in the first round of his first Wimbledon and then went on to win seven titles there. Now how could he lose the first round on a grass court with that serve? The reason is, he wasn't comfortable in that situation. Sampras also played the

French Open every year and only made it past the quarterfinals once. I'm sure as time went on, he felt more comfortable playing in Paris, but the environment (the slow clay court and heavy, slow balls) did not favor his game.

You might not be fortunate enough to choose between Sydney and Tokyo, but you can choose between two local parks. Which one best suits your style of play? Where do you feel most comfortable? The answer to those questions can be the difference between winning and losing.

Tip #79: Know the ball.

The ball matters. It's as important as the string and tension of your racket. Over 50 different tennis balls are on the world market. Use the ball that best suits your style of play. If you play a slow, countering game, why use a light, hard ball that suits your opponent's big serve?

If you don't know what type of ball suits your style, then go online and buy a couple different kinds of balls and use them in practice to see which ones you should bring to your league or tournament matches. Or, you can simply call a tennis ball supplier and ask them the characteristics of each ball. Lots of tournaments require that you bring your own can of balls with you, with the winner taking the can of balls that wasn't used. However, most competitive tournaments have an assigned ball. Try to find out what it is. It's important. A tennis match can come down to one or two points, and knowing what balls will be used can make the difference.

The Internet has made getting such information a lot easier. Online reviews will tell you how various balls play. To get a feel for what to expect at a tournament, you should at least hit with the tournament balls once before play begins.

Tip #80: Know the supervisor's name and make sure that he knows yours.

Can you imagine not knowing your boss' name? Well, as far a competitive match is concerned, the tournament director is your boss. Just as your boss has the power to fire you, the tournament director can default you.

Recently in Mexico, I was playing in 110-degree heat. The tournament director was a grumpy man named Juan who stayed indoors all day, smoking Marlboro reds. Everybody thought he was a jerk, but while playing in the qualifying, I took a few minutes every day to say hello and gradually got to know him. I could see he wanted to help the players who respected the time and effort he was putting into the tournament. By the time I qualified for the main draw, I was exhausted. I needed rest and Juan made sure that I got it, scheduling me to play my next three matches at night. No heat and no humidity, which was huge for my game. After losing in the semifinals, I stopped in Juan's office to say thanks. He told me that it was pleasure to meet a tennis player that actually treated him as a normal person and not just another boring director.

The tournament director holds your fate in the palm of his hand. Make sure that you know him, thank him, and greet him at every chance possible. Players don't understand the long hours it takes to put on a tournament and coordinate all the match times and courts. Of a 128 draw, I bet 120 of the players don't know the tournament director's name. Be one of the eight players that does and maybe you'll get better treatment, like I did. The players that don't know the supervisor are at a disadvantage. It's not a computer that puts together the schedule, the match courts, the housing, the transportation, and everything else that goes into planning a competitive event. It's a person who likes to be acknowledged for the work he has done. If you treat that person with respect, he'll usually do whatever he can to help you. In Mexico, Juan helped me play better tennis.

Tip #81: Speak confidently about your game and your chances to others.

"Man, tomorrow I play the first seed. I think I'll book my flight for the afternoon." Sound familiar? I have never been to any tournament, at any level, without hearing insecure comments from competitors. A coach of mine used to say that 99 percent of the draw is already determined before the matches are played. The things you say around a tournament matter. Do you think Andre Agassi runs around the tournament on the first day talking to everyone about his draw?

Stay composed and don't give a thing away. If you meet somebody new, be friendly, but keep in mind that he wants you to lose. Away from the tournament, have as much fun as you want. However, the courts are your office, your place of work.

Whether you realize it or not, your words are your thoughts and your beliefs, and they determine your fate. "I got the worst draw," you tell a few players over lunch. "I play the fourth seed in the first round. Do you know if they have a back draw at this tournament?" Sound familiar? These comments expose your thoughts and your fate. Is playing the fourth seed really that bad? To win a tournament, you'll have to play good players. A seed is nothing but red ink instead of black. If the fourth seed was really that amazing, the tournament would be named after him. By asking about a consolation draw, you are simply guaranteeing that you will be playing in it.

Speak confidently. You'll not only convince others you're a good player, you'll convince yourself. I'm not telling you to stand on a table and scream, "I'm going to beat all of you." However, the next time somebody asks about your draw or an opponent, just say it's going to be a great match and that you're going to compete hard.

Muhammad Ali spoke with such confidence in front of the world that he began to believe that he was just what he was saying, the best boxer in the world. You can do the same. The next time you face a tough opponent, go somewhere alone and look in the mirror. Make sure that you are making eye contact with yourself and then say, "I am going to win in straight sets." Or, if you would rather stay away from result oriented goals, say, "I am certain that I will compete with intensity and tenacity." Your words determine your fate, so choose your words carefully, but confidently.

Tip #82: Accept the draw.

What happens when the draw comes out? Everybody stands around it thinking, "Okay, I'll lose to her in the third round," or, "Yeah, I'll get to the semis before losing to John again."

You scan across the poster until you see a name that you think will beat you, and then you decide if that's a "good" or "bad" place to lose as far as your expectations are concerned. If it's a "good" place then you have a "good draw," and if it's a "bad" place then you have a "bad draw." I put all those in quotation marks because a good loss or bad loss, or a "good draw" or a "bad draw" don't exist. The draw does not determine who'll win the tournament or who'll lose. It's just a random drawing of all the players that have entered. The seeds that are placed in the draw are only seeded because of their past performances. However, the past is history.

Stop talking about the draw. What good does it do? Look at one thing: who you're playing against, not if you or your opponent are seeded. Not who you'll be playing in the second round. Deal with the rest of it when it comes. Focus on the task at hand. The draw won't change. The only thing that can change is your attitude about it. The sooner you accept the draw, the sooner you can think about what's important: match preparation, meals, warm-up, and competing. You have no better opportunity than the next match, no matter who you play, to become a better player.

Michael Bradley/Getty Images

Take a look at who you play next round and then leave the draw alone.

Tip #83: Let others complain.

Tennis players love to complain. Following are 10 common tennis complaints and my responses to each of them.

Complaint #1: "This tournament site is terrible."

Response: It is a privilege to play tennis and compete and have fun. Other people around the world are fighting in wars and working the farm. Would you rather be playing a tennis match at a sub-par country club or milking the cows at 5 a.m.?

Complaint #2: "The balls are terrible."

Response: You knew what the balls were before you got to the tournament. Complain then, not now. If you didn't know what the balls were before you got to the tournament, then you should only be mad at yourself. See Tip #79 ("Know the ball").

Complaint #3: "I have the worst draw."

Response: See Tip #82 ("Accept the draw"). The only reason you have a bad draw is because you think you do. The person you play thinks they have a great draw because they heard you complaining in the lobby earlier.

Complaint #4: "It's impossible to play well when I am injured."

Response: If you are injured, then don't sign up for the tournament. If you do decide to play, then make no excuses after the match. If you step onto the court, you have no excuses. I have seen players in eastern Europe win matches with a dislocated shoulder, so if you think your blister is an injury, think again.

Complaint #5: "The umpires are terrible."

Response: The umpires are either volunteering or getting paid very little to be here. Maybe they made some mistakes, but then again, if you practiced more, you wouldn't be in such a close match. Plus, if you thank them for working the tournament instead of complaining to them, you will find that they happen to make some mistakes in your favor. They are doing the best they can, and you have to accept that fact.

Complaint #6: "If I was just winning I would be able to do what my coach wants."

Response: If you do what your coach wants, you will win. People always think, "If I just." "If I just won this match, I would be happy," "If I just had a better coach I would be winning," "If I just was from down south I would play better outdoors." You are where you are for a reason, so take responsibility for the current ranking or position you are in now. Everything comes down to you, not your coach.

Complaint #7: "I have never stayed in a hotel this bad."

Response: If you are complaining about the hotel you are staying in, then you need to try not staying in one and compare the difference. I have been very fortunate to have enough money to usually stay in hotels, but I have had those late nights where I could not get a room or was stranded someplace where I had to "improvise." Does your room have a bed? Is a roof over your head? Then it's fine. I have played some great tennis by sleeping on the floor the night before.

Complaint #8: "I hate playing at 8 a.m."

Response: The best way to make sure you play well in the morning is to wake up early enough. Do not make the excuse that you are not a morning match player. You need to find a way to play well in the morning, and odds are, it simply means waking up earlier and getting your body moving. Whenever my brother would play at 8 a.m., he would play an entire practice set before his first match. What a great way to make sure you are going to play well.

Complaint #9: "The weather makes it impossible to play well."

Response: I have talked about the weather before, so you know what I am going to say: Tip #12 ("Accept the weather"). It can definitely be a test, but keep in mind that "champions adjust." How much adversity can you handle?

Complaint #10: "The courts are so bad."

Response: Sometimes the courts will be bad. If you have a good serve and a good volley, then the ball doesn't need to bounce on your side for you to hold serve.

Just by listening to these complaints, you are putting your mind and your game into a negative state. Let others complain, while you focus on winning.

Tip #84: Listen more and talk less to other players.

You can be popular at your school or away from the courts. At the tournament site, popularity shouldn't be your concern. Keep quiet and listen to what your competition has to say. You can learn a lot from them and improve your chances.

On the pro tour, players have to show up between the hours of 7 and 9 p.m. the day before the start of the tournament and sign in for the qualifying draw. It is a very social event, with almost everyone standing around and talking to one another—everyone except the top players. They get in and get out. They know that the more they talk with their competitors, the more their competitors will begin to feel comfortable with them.

Listen to what the other players are talking about. Listen to what the umpires are talking about. Listen to what the tournament director and the coaches are saying. I remember getting ready for a match in Switzerland. I was playing a Canadian player that I knew very little about. All I knew was what he looked like. After a practice session, I went to the lounge area and was stretching alone when I saw him on the phone, his back to me. "Yeah, he's a serve and volleyer," he was saying. "Yeah I know, I'm going to hit some extra forehands in the morning. He likes to serve to my backhand, which is good. His forehand is worse, so I'll serve there on the big points. He's a good competitor, but I'll try to get him upset..."

What did I learn? Everything. It couldn't have worked out any better. The next day I showed up, attacked his forehand, served to his forehand, volleyed, expected forehands returns on big points, and was a mental rock because I knew that he was going to try to get me upset. I won 6-2, 6-1.

Tennis players will talk until they're blue in the face. They'll talk about matches they've won and lost, about certain players that drive them crazy, their injuries, their weaknesses, their past results, their fears, their reaction to pressure, etc. It's not rude to listen. In fact, most players will like you more. It's amazing what other players will tell you about their game.

By doing less talking and more listening, you'll learn valuable information from the tournament director (court playability, starting times, good restaurants, stringing), the umpire (affect of the weather on court, vision on the court, players to be wary of), and from other players (their weaknesses, reasons for losing, their competitive nature, injuries, attitude, and fitness levels). All of this information adds up to a huge competitive advantage.

Tip #85: Recognize how other players view you.

How do you want other players to view you? Do you want to be known as the funny, happy-go-lucky guy? Do you want to be known as the cheater? As the player with amazing talent but terrible work ethic? Before you walk into a tournament environment, you should answer those questions. If you don't, other players will do it for you. They'll label you, and that label can stick. Like it or not, your image is important.

When I was first learning to play tennis, I was always laughing around the courts. I was the joker. Only when I started to play tournaments did this reputation begin to hurt me. My opponents liked me, but didn't respect my game. After beating me, they'd want me to joke with them. I had to change my image. I wanted to have the image of a player, a champion, and a hard worker. So, I changed the way I was on court. I didn't change my personality off the court. I still liked to horse around, but not on the tennis court.

Tennis is supposed to be fun, and if you're not having fun, then you need to reconsider why you're playing. I still make jokes on the court and laugh at tournaments, but I do it a lot less. I know players who have every shot in the book, with a 130-mph serve and amazing athleticism, yet they get no respect from anyone because they're considered a "goof," a "head case," or a "tanker." I also know players who are four-foot nothing, with weak serves, no volleys, and braces all over their body, yet they demand respect from every player in the tournament because they're the "workhorse," the "overachiever," the "aggressive competitor," or an "animal."

If you have your opponents' respect because of the way that you practice and conduct yourself, you start the match with an advantage. I generally don't care what other people think of me, but I do when it can determine whether or not I win or lose a tennis match.

The following are a couple of easy ways to change or just improve your image around the tournament:

- Practice before everyone else does. Be the first person on the court, finishing your practice as other players are just walking into the site. Hit on a court where others will see you practicing, your competition will take notice.

- The same goes for Tip #59 ("Practice after a loss to immediately feel better"). You gain your opponents' respect not only for the upcoming back draw, but also for the next tournament.

- While competing, be an animal, but a composed animal. It's great to be intense, but don't lose matches because of anger.

- When you're not playing or practicing, keep quiet around the tournament. You don't have to be a mute, but know who your true friends are. A little bit of mystery is good. If the other players around the tournament aren't quite sure what to think of you, you've gotten in their head.

Tip #86: Spend money on anything tennis related.

Anything that is tennis-related, such as stringing, eating, sleeping, preparation, travel, equipment, etc., is worth the money. Don't kick yourself if you need new shoes or your racket restrung. Take care of everything that can affect the way you play, and by doing so, you will earn mental calmness while competing. On the other hand, you should limit when you spend money on things that aren't tennis related (junk food, alcohol, cigarettes, casinos, and any activity that keeps you staying up late).

I have seen players take their prize money and head straight to the casino, or, even worse, come home at 3 a.m. from the casino when they play the next day. I've been with players who have called and asked their parents to deposit money into their bank account, only to take their ATM card and go straight to the casinos, strip clubs, or shopping mall.

Most tennis players have a lot of money. It's possible to be a great player without all that money. However, players with greater resources of coaching, courts, and training facilities have an undeniable advantage. Regardless of your resources, it's important to spend money on things that are tennis related while economizing in all other areas. You'll know that you've covered all the necessary bases to compete at your best and that you've been disciplined about it.

Tip #87: Stop giving away your secrets.

Are there really any huge secrets in tennis? Yes. This book is filled with them. Use these "secrets" to your advantage, but don't tell everyone about them. If you've given something away, don't complain when you lose. That's tennis and that's life.

7

Mental/Physical Preparation

Tip #88: Read more.

Tip #89: Visualize and monitor your responses.

Tip #90: Carry water at all times.

Tip #91: Develop a rehab program that you do every day.

Tip #92: Take days off.

Tip #93: Keep a journal of your practices and matches.

Tip #94: Don't waste your time by checking other people's results.

Tip #95: Take vitamin C (antioxidants) during a competition.

Tip #96: Meditate.

Tip #97: Memorize the word "perseverance."

Tip #98: Read post-match press conferences of top players.

Tip #99: Understand luck.

Tip #100: Get fit to gain confidence.

Tip #101: Read "Enjoy the Moment" by Stewart Doyle.

Everybody talks about the importance of the mental game, from TV commentators to the players in the tournament. However, almost nobody is working on their mental game. You're only as good as your mind, so start improving it today. Work on ways to feel confident, composed, and cool under pressure. If you think that some people have it and some people don't, you are wrong. Mental strength, like physical strength, can be acquired through constant work. I include physical preparation in this section because physical fitness and mental confidence go hand in hand.

Make a commitment to identifying and actually doing something about one of your mental weaknesses. Just five minutes of mental exercises every day can make a huge difference.

Tip #88: Read more.

I have yet to meet a tennis player that spends more time reading than talking or watching TV. It seems to be a prerequisite that if you play tennis or any sport, you have to be glued to the TV. Turn it off. Read a book.

Books like *The Power of Now* by Eckhart Tolle, and *The Seven Spiritual Laws of Success* by Deepak Chopra were not written with tennis in mind. They were written more as a manual on how to think, act, and live life. However, they do teach you how to accept any challenge and respond to any adversity.

The Power of Now shows what a nuisance our memory can be. Who we are is not defined by what we have done in the past, but by what we are doing now. Understanding this idea can make all the difference in your tennis game. If you could completely forget the past, you'd be free to play tennis as it was intended, freely and clearly. Tolle tells us to stop thinking. Nothing really exists except for this actual moment. Learning to live in the present moment will have an amazing effect not only on your tennis, but also on your life.

Chopra's book is a quick read, very short and concise, instructing readers how to step back from their goals and let things evolve, which he calls "the law of detachment" and "the law of least effort." The best way to win is to stop caring if you win. Stop working so hard. To accomplish more, do less. Coaches around the country tell juniors that in order to play good tennis they have to practice relentlessly. I've learned that you do need to practice, but two hours is as good as six. Tennis academies around the world spend millions of dollars trying to develop top level pros, yet how much time and energy is put into their mental game? Use these two books to help your mind while competing and you will see a dramatic improvement.

Tip #89: Visualize and monitor your responses.

Practicing visualization should be part of your daily ritual. Simple visualization techniques can be used to improve your practices, matches, and technique.

What percentage of your sport is mental? Virtually every high level athlete will say that their sport is mostly mental. Yet what percentage of their practice time do athletes spend on training the mental part of their game? Almost none. As a tennis player, you have to train your mind just as you train your body.

Close your eyes and imagine it's 4-4 in the first set, 30-all. You hit a winner on the line and your opponent calls it out. What do you do? Do you panic? Do you scream and yell and lose the next point and set? Do you maintain your composure? Do you get pumped and play better and save the break point and win the set? What is your response to the adversity? By going through that situation right now, the next time you're actually faced with something like it, you'll respond the right way.

When I was 19 years old, I had surgery on my right wrist and was in a cast for six weeks. Unable to hold a racket, I still practiced every day. I worked on my movement, my volley form, my serve, my ability to play better under pressure, and my return. I did these actions all in my head. I never stepped one foot on the court. When the six weeks were over, I discovered that parts of my game had actually improved. The power of the mind to visualize and fix problems is astonishing.

Just like ground strokes and serves, your mental game will need constant work. Don't be discouraged if you don't get it right way. Odds are you've never trained your brain in this way, so start slow, as if you were lifting weights for the first time. Eventually you can play a whole set in your mind. As you do, use all five senses. It makes what you're imagining more real. Imagine the courts, the color of the fences and backdrops, the sun, the clouds, the sound of the ball coming off the strings, you and your opponents' grunts, the distractions, what you're eating and drinking at changeovers, the smell of the balls, the feel of your racket at impact, the feel of the surface on your feet, etc.

If you're having a tough time getting started, put some music on, preferably music with no words. Sit alone with no distractions. Close your eyes (unless you're driving) and picture a challenging situation. Do you often blow leads in first sets? Then pretend its 5-3 in the first set. Play out the rest of the set. Be realistic. Don't hit winner after winner; instead, visualize how you'll react to mistakes. Even without stepping on the court, visualization can correct technical mistakes in your game. Your brain will see the right way to do something over a course of many visualization sessions.

Tip #90: Carry water at all times.

We all know that you're supposed to drink eight tall glasses of water a day to properly hydrate your body. If you're playing a lot of tennis or working out, you'll need to be drinking nearly double that amount. The best way to stay hydrated is to carry a bottle of water with you at all times. It's a habit you need to develop if you want to make sure you are capable of playing your best tennis.

Most Americans are dehydrated. We drink way too much soda, coffee, and fruit juice. Water is what our body needs, not sugars, caffeine, and carbs. Don't think that because you drink five Snapples a day you are hydrated. You're filling your body with sugars when it needs water. Water provides lubricants to our joints, helps regulate body temperature, and keeps your mind sharp during a match. When your body is dehydrated, you make mental errors and your body fatigues faster.

The average male tennis player sweats out about three liters of sweat an hour in warm and humid conditions (a little less for a female). The human body can only take in about one liter of water an hour comfortably. So even if you are drinking water during your match, you'll still be dehydrated, which means you need to replenish your fluids off the courts.

Of course, you'll have to use the bathroom a lot more, which is something you'll just have to learn to deal with it. The point is, you want to be hydrated all of the time, not just during matches or practices. If you have a tough workout or match, it's important to not only drink water, but also add some sodium and electrolytes to your drink (Gatorade is a great choice). Stay away from sports drinks that have caffeine or carbonation.

Tip #91: Develop a rehab program that you do every day.

You're always at risk of getting injured. Whether you're playing great or poorly, you need to prepare your body to handle the stress that comes from competing. An injury is seldom the player's fault. However, every player has to ask themselves what he can do to better prepare his body for the stress of competition. What part of your body have you consistently had trouble with? Your knees? Your shoulder? Your back? The more tennis you play, the greater the risk of hurting yourself. Take the bull by the horns and develop a rehab program that you can do every day to minimize risk.

To compete knowing that you've taken care of your biggest physical weakness is great for your confidence. If you have no physical barriers in your way, you have nothing stopping you from achieving your tennis goals.

I recommend starting your day with the rehab program. For me, I always woke up and did five minutes of ankle strengthening exercises every morning. My ankles have always been the weakest part of my body. Identify one part of your body that needs to be stronger. Even if you feel great now and haven't had an injury in years, think back to when you did experience some difficulty. Odds are, that's the part of the body that'll get injured first.

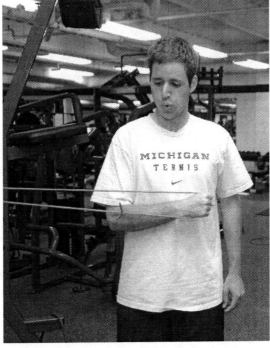

Just five minutes a day of injury prevention can keep you healthy for years.

Tip #92: Take days off.

The average club player isn't able to practice every day. However, taking days off doesn't only apply to those who play every day of the week. Everybody, especially juniors, need to be very careful about getting burned out or injured.

Some athletes think a day off means sitting on the couch with a Coke in one hand and a Pepsi in the other. A day off means an active day off. You're up and moving, taking care of errands, maybe taking the dog for a longer walk than normal. If you do nothing, you'll have a harder time coming back the next day. Relax by being active. At the same time, make sure you're enjoying your day off.

Be wary of a coach who doesn't understand the importance of taking days off. People often say they play surprisingly well after a long time off, which is not a coincidence. They've recharged their batteries, mental and physical.

Taking a day off should be as much a part of your weekly schedule as hitting serves and returns. Are you a little tired of playing twice a week? Do you get frustrated on the court too easily? Well then, get off the court. You'll play your best tennis when you want to be on the court. Top pros take weeks away from the game. They're still staying fit and working in the gym or playing other sports to keep sharp, but they might not pick up a racket for four weeks. Ivan Lendl used to take his family to Colorado and ride a bike in the mountains for four weeks to stay fit, and he wouldn't even bring a tennis racket. Andre Agassi takes weeks away from the courts to remain fresh for the few tournaments he does play. So why are you so worried about taking a measly two days off from the game? Even if you don't play every day, skipping your weekly hit can help your game. If you feel your tennis game has deteriorated and you're searching for a reason to play, take a few weeks off. After the second week, you'll miss playing, come back excited, and hitting the ball well.

Tip #93: Keep a journal of your practices and matches.

I have kept a journal for over six years. What could I possibly write about tennis on a daily basis for six years? Practice drills I liked, feelings I had on the court, progress that I've made, weaknesses that needed to be worked on, scores of matches, weaknesses that certain players have, new strings I've tried, new tensions, injuries, weight programs, footwork drills, scheduling ideas, doubles concepts, fears I have, motivational phrases, etc. Basically everything.

I often look back at my old journals and see how much progress I've made. I might feel frustrated after a bad practice, but with my journal, I can look back to another tough day and quickly realize that as long as I'm working hard, I'll achieve my goals.

So many players spend exorbitant amounts of money on private lessons and then walk off the court and never think about them. If they sat down for only five minutes after a lesson and wrote down their observations, they'd see an immediate improvement in their game.

Keeping a daily journal is most helpful when you're playing poorly, when it seems nothing is going right. The journal can help you find the answer to your problems. You can look back to when you were playing well and see what you were doing differently. You might notice patterns of when you peak athletically. Without writing down your daily or even weekly tennis thoughts and activities, you will be lost.

A journal provides a sense of direction. To know where you're going, it helps to know where you've been.

Wolverine Photo/Amir Gamzu

Always write down your thoughts and observations of your game.

Tip #94: Don't waste your time by checking other people's results.

One drawback to the Internet is that it makes it too easy to obsess over results and rankings. Get off the computer and onto the practice court. Too many players, old and young, spend way too much time looking at other people's results. "Wow, Bill beat Paul," they think. "Paul beat Jim, Jim beat Todd, and Todd's younger brother won the back draw at nationals. So that means I am a national champion." The only place where you can determine if you're better than somebody is the court. Checking results is a waste of time.

Do you think the top players check the Internet to see who is winning and who is losing? When they're out of a tournament, it's over as far as they're concerned and the other players' results mean nothing.

I used to sit in front of the tennis web pages and check all the results around the world. I'd see this guy was playing well, this guy pulled out with an injury, this guy lost to a bad player—all of this information was doing nothing but altering my opinion of my own game and abilities. The fact is, you don't know anything about a player until you're standing across the net from him competing in a match.

Successful players never compare themselves to others. They let their competitors bring out their best, but that's as far as it goes. They don't worry about how much media attention, publicity, or popularity a certain athlete gets. If you too can keep other people's results from having any effect on you, you'll become a better tennis player. The best way to do so is to not even bother knowing the results.

However, you should support your teammates. If you're on a tennis team, hoping that a teammate loses so you'll look better only communicates insecurity. Others pick up on that weakness. Also, it takes enormous energy being negative and unsupportive. It can suck away your passion and enthusiasm for the sport. Other people's results are for other people, not you.

Tip #95: Take vitamin C (antioxidants) during a competition.

Ever noticed how after playing a lot of long and competitive matches, you feel a little sick? This feeling can even happen after a tough week of practice or even a few days of four hour hits when you're normally used to only two hours. The immune system is getting pushed to its limit, and eventually, it doesn't have enough strength to fight off illness. It's for this reason that, while competing in a tournament, I take a 1,000 mg tablet of vitamin C and a 222 IU tablet of vitamin E.

If you want proof your body is working extra hard during a tournament, try the following: take your heart rate one morning after you wake up but are still lying in bed (after a tough day of matches the day before). Now, take your heart rate the day after a rest day. You'll see quite a difference.

If your morning heart rate is higher than normal, your immune system is weaker than normal. You need rest. You also need Vitamins C and E. Both are members of the antioxidant vitamin family, thwarting the chain reaction of "free radicals" that harm your body. Drinking orange juice with breakfast is not enough. You need to supply your body with ample amounts of the "C" and "E" to seriously help your body recover from a tough week.

Tip #96: Meditate.

The average tennis player stands on the court with about as much mental and physical ease as a mouse in a mousetrap. Relax. You're in control—or, you should be. The reason players stand on the court so tensed up is they don't know how to stop it. If they begin to practice mediation, they'll feel an amazing change. It will all seem so simple.

Meditation coordinates the mind and body. It begins with your breathing. The deeper and longer you can take one single breath, the more relaxed you'll be. Sit alone, silently, and in an upright position for at least five minutes every day. If you lie down or slouch, you might find your five-minute meditation turns into a 45-minute nap. Take deep nasal breaths, long and slow. Try to clear your mind. Don't be upset if you're not able to at first. Your brain may race in a hundred different directions, but just be patient, you will get better at it. Even just sitting quietly for five minutes a day helps. Eventually, "slipping into the void" becomes easier. Through practice, the mind will quiet down.

The effect meditation can have on your tennis is both subtle and profound. Your game becomes smoother, less rigid. You start to get feelings of being in the "zone," where you can do nothing wrong and perfect shots seem to fly off your racket. Your mind is clear. It isn't focused on winning, winning, winning. It's just being.

Tip #97: Memorize the word "perseverance."

Perseverance means "refusing to be discouraged by obstacles or difficulties, continuing steadily with courage and patience." Tennis is a sport of second chances. You'll almost always have another opportunity to beat a player that beat you. The key is perseverance. You might lose the closest, toughest, and hardest match of your life. However, if you wake up the next day with motivation to give it another try, you'll succeed in the end.

In the first tournament I ever played, I lost 6-0, 6-0. I cried all the way home. However, the next day I was on the court playing and practicing. Players have badly lost their professional debut only to go on to win major championships.

Memorize the definition of perseverance. Is any word more important? You can either mope or you can persevere. If you persevere long enough, you are guaranteed success. "Never give up," Winston Churchill said, "Never, never, never, never give up." Repeat the definition every day until the words roll out of your mouth every time you're faced with adversity. Write the definition down. Tape it to your bathroom mirror or on the refrigerator. If you consistently devote your game and development to those words, you are guaranteed success on and off the court.

If you persevere long enough, you are guaranteed success.

Tip #98: Read post-match press conferences of top players.

Through the Internet, you can find the post-match press conferences of the best players in the world. No longer do you have to be sitting in the pressroom to hear what Roger Federer, Serena Williams, Justine Henin-Hardenne, Andy Roddick, and Andre Agassi said about their last match. All you have to do is find the official website of the tournament and go to the "press" section. All four grand slam websites offer this feature, as do many other tour events. The grand slam websites are:

Australian Open = www.ausopen.org

French Open = www.rolandgarros.com

Wimbledon = www.wimbledon.org

US Open = www.usopen.org

These players know what they're doing and it behooves the rest of us to learn from them. One thing you'll learn is that they experience the same range of emotions we all do. They just handle them better.

Take a look at Andy Roddick's (or any other top player's) post-match press conferences, especially after a tough loss. He always says the same thing—that if he does the right things throughout the course of the year, he'll eventually have great results. He doesn't berate himself and isn't afraid to talk about his match.

Stop looking at the results of the last tournament you played and start reading what the great players have to say. Learn how to think as they do.

Tip #99: Understand luck.

After winning the Michigan High School State championship my sophomore year in high school, I got a nice letter from a coach I worked with. "Luck comes when preparation meets opportunity," he wrote. I remember when I first read that sentence, I felt as if everything finally made sense. I had just played some remarkable tennis and achieved something that I didn't entirely feel ready for. I wouldn't say that I got lucky, but I did feel that luck had a hand in my success that weekend, and I would argue that it has a hand in every athlete's success. However, that coach pointed out that any amount of luck I received, I earned through my hard work. To be lucky, you need to be doing the right things.

Most tennis players don't understand luck. They think it'll just fall in their lap and make them a great player. In fact, it works the other way around. First, you have to become a great tennis player and then you'll get lucky.

Luck is a part of your success and will come to you when you have prepared yourself to be successful without luck. You have to be persistent enough to make opportunities for yourself. When you finally get them, you have to make sure you're prepared to take the challenge. Only then will luck be on your side.

I have lost a lot of unlucky matches. I have had players pass me at net with let cord winners and shank lobs over my head on break points. I once had a bee sting me in the face just as I was about to go for a crucial overhead. However, the more tennis I play, the more I understand that luck comes and goes. If you're on the up side of luck and haven't been working on your game or have had a poor attitude, your luck will only take you so far. However, if you're motivated and fully prepared, when luck falls upon you, you'll be ready to do great things. A good run of luck has carried hard workers a lot farther than lazy players.

Luck comes when preparation meets opportunity.

Brian Bahr/Getty Images

Tip #100: Get fit to gain confidence.

Being fit has no substitution. Fitness breeds confidence. If you're struggling to make anything positive happen, if you're afraid to compete and are tentative on the court, then I recommend you put the racket down and lace up the running shoes.

Getting fit hurts. It's tough. It requires personal discipline and guts. It's not fun. However, by getting more fit, you'll reach deep down into your gut and pull out all the talent and hustle within. It's up to you.

Nobody but you can make it happen. Players often tell me, "I need a coach to make me run on the track," or, "I do better if someone is motivating me while I run." Nonsense. The more you can effectively push yourself, by yourself, the tougher you will become. You make the biggest mental gains when you are alone. Just you and the track, the weight room, or the stadium stairs. If you can develop the mental toughness to make yourself do what hurts alone, you will improve your game by leaps and bounds.

In addition to doing specific exercises and drills to improve your tennis game, you should also do exercises that test your heart and your guts, that have nothing to do with tennis per se, except making you tougher. Your brain will try to talk you out of doing what you know you have to. What will your choice be? Will you wimp out and take it easy or will you be the Army sergeant in your ear, telling you to go harder and faster?

Getting fit might not be fun, but nothing is more rewarding and exciting then stepping onto the tennis court after four weeks of tough fitness, knowing you've got your confidence back.

Fitness has no shortcuts. You might be able to pop a few big serves now and again on a tennis court to get yourself out of trouble, but if you want to get fit, no easy equivalent exists.

Tennis is an anaerobic activity, a "start and stop" sport. It requires short bursts of speed for the length of the point. You are then given 25 seconds to rest before doing it again. The biggest mistake tennis players make when they want to get fit is they do not model their training on an actual tennis match. You want to do exercises that are similar in time and speed as a tennis match. Playing basketball is a great way to get more fit for tennis. It requires starting and stopping, jumping, and proper footwork. It requires small bursts of speed and then short breaks as you jog down the court. Sprints are also effective. Run a 30-second sprint and then take a minute off, or run a 10-second sprint and take 20 seconds off. Have your sprints be the "points" with the break being the time between points. Swimming laps for two hours at a slow and steady pace will definitely help your overall stamina, but it won't improve your speed and recovery time. It might even make you slower. The workout doesn't have to be long to be effective. A half-hour of plyometric training, involving different jumps and sprints, will leave you completely spent.

If you want to learn more about plyometric training, a lot of books are available on the subject. Basically, it simulates your actions on the tennis court. So, do three sets of 10 squat jumps (hands on head, squat down, and jump as high as you can) followed by a 10-meter sprint after the last jump. In time, you'll be more explosive, powerful on the court, able to play longer points, and recover more quickly.

It all comes down to making a personal commitment. For some people, this commitment might mean working out six days a week for an hour. For others, it will mean simply taking a 30-minute walk three times a week. Whatever the case may be, do not underestimate the correlation between fitness and your confidence on and off the court.

Brian Bahr/Getty Images

It's important to be agile and fit, which come from years of doing exercises that mimic the movement on the court.

Tip #101: Read "Enjoy the Moment" by Stewart Doyle.

My freshman year at the University of Illinois, we had an assistant coach named Stewart Doyle. Doyle had a remarkable ability to relate to the mind of a tennis player. He knew exactly what you were thinking on the court. He understood the emotions, fears, and excitements associated with being in a tight match. A match does not come down to who is more athletically gifted, who has the best racket, or the best past results. It comes down to whose mind is stronger. It sounds silly, but I never knew that fact. Before I met Doyle, I thought that tennis was more physical than mental.

It was hours before our first match in the NCAAs that Stewart handed me a piece of paper and told me to read it before I went to bed. It said:

Enjoy the moment (how good is life right now)
What lies ahead is totally up to you.
Why look back and think that when I was in
My physical prime of youth that I just didn't
Totally live it.

If you go for it and fail, it hurts
       Temporarily (All you can ever do is go for it)

If you don't go for it and fail, it hurts
       Permanently

What does this mean?

It means you must always be brave
Brave enough to do everything in your power to
prepare for competition.
Brave enough to mentally channel all your energies
until your mind feels empty.
Brave enough to fight forever, even if one of
the outcomes could be death.

                The Battlefield is set
        If you are brave in all these areas
                The battle will be beautiful
                You will be a Hero.

Not only did this message help me the next day, but it has helped me in every day that has followed. I hope it inspires you as much as it did me.

Have fun. You'll play better, enjoy it more, and of course, win more.

Conclusion

By far, the most important characteristic of any tennis player at any level is his attitude. I have seen players of all abilities, heights, shapes, and sizes in every part of the world and the simple truth is that those players with a positive mental attitude win more, period. Every single one of these tips becomes completely meaningless if you choose to poison yourself with negative thoughts. I say "choose" because it is a choice to be negative, nothing more. The opposite is also true. You can choose to have a positive attitude.

Ironically, in the sport of tennis, the better you become, the simpler the game is. I used to think tennis was so complicated. However, as I won more and more and the years of hard work started paying off, I learned that it was quite a simple game. Compared to the winner of grand slam titles, I've still got a ways to go. However, I'm still learning and still improving, and every day parts of my game become even simpler. The same will happen to you—if you stay with it. Tennis will become easier. You'll have more fun. Now get out and do it.

About the Author

Michael Kosta currently teaches tennis independently nationwide. Previously, he served as the assistant men's tennis coach at the University of Michigan for two years. He now works with the Wolverines team as a volunteer assistant coach when he is in town. Michael played on the professional tennis tour for three years, reaching world rankings in the top 900 in singles and the top 350 in doubles. Prior to his professional career, Michael earned a degree in speech communications from the University of Illinois, where he played four years on the number one nationally ranked tennis team and established himself as one of the nation's top singles and doubles players. Michael, a two-time Michigan High School State Champion, is a PTR certified teaching pro as well as a Level 1 USTA High Performance graduate. He is single and resides in Ann Arbor, Michigan.